All the Fighting They Want

THE ATLANTA CAMPAIGN
FROM PEACHTREE CREEK TO THE CITY'S SURRENDER
JULY 18-SEPTEMBER 2, 1864

by Stephen Davis

EMERGING CIVIL WAR SERIES

Chris Mackowski, series editor
Kristopher D. White, chief historian

Also part of the Emerging Civil War Series:

All the Fighting They Want

THE ATLANTA CAMPAIGN
FROM PEACHTREE CREEK TO THE CITY'S SURRENDER
JULY 18-SEPTEMBER 2, 1864

by Stephen Davis

EMERGING CIVIL WAR SERIES

SB
Savas Beatie
California

First edition, first printing

ISBN-13 (paperback): 978-1-61121-319-5
ISBN-13 (ebook): 978-1-61121-320-1

Library of Congress Cataloging-in-Publication Data

Names: Davis, Stephen, 1948- author.
Title: All the fighting they want : the Atlanta Campaign from Peach Tree Creek to the surrender, July 18-September 2, 1864 / by Stephen Davis.
Description: First edition. | El Dorado Hills, California : Savas Beattie, 2017. | Series: Emerging Civil War series
Identifiers: LCCN 2016014466| ISBN 9781611213195 (pbk) | ISBN 9781611213201 (ebk.)
Subjects: LCSH: Atlanta Campaign, 1864.
Classification: LCC E476.7 .D375 2017 | DDC 973.7/371--dc23
LC record available at https://lccn.loc.gov/2016014466

Published by
Savas Beatie LLC
989 Governor Drive, Suite 102
El Dorado Hills, California 95762
Phone: 916-941-6896
Email: sales@savasbeatie.com
Web: www.savasbeatie.com

Savas Beatie titles are available at special discounts for bulk purchases in the United States by corporations, institutions, and other organizations. For more details, please contact Special Sales, P.O. Box 4527, El Dorado Hills, CA 95762, or you may e-mail us at sales@savasbeatie.com, or visit our website at www.savasbeatie.com for additional information.

MIX
Paper from
responsible sources
FSC® C011935

*To the late great Bell Irvin Wiley (1906-1980),
who taught me that writing clearly about
what you know is just as important as
knowing it in the first place.*

Table of Contents

The Windsor Smith House served as Hood's headquarters. Today, the site is merely a vacant lot. (ahc)

List of Maps

Maps by Hal Jespersen

Acknowledgments

For this contribution to the Emerging Civil War Series, I thank Dr. Chris Mackowski, series editor, for his prudent oversight and patient accommodation as we labored toward publication.

Hannah Gordon laid the whole thing out, bless her heart—a phrase she doesn't hear enough in upstate New York.

The Nash Farm battlefield, located in Hampton, Georgia, is operated and staffed by the Friends of Nash Farm, Inc. The museum, open most Fridays and Saturdays except for holidays, houses a large artifact collection, period clothing exhibits, and history of the Nash farm and family. (nf)

Hal Jesperson continues to work his cartographic magic, and it's getting to be that any Civil War author whose book his work appears in feels most fortunate indeed.

Talk about the tail wagging the dog: Gordon Jones's and Gould Hagler's appendixes add value to this work which far exceeds their appended essays. Gordon has become the internationally renowned expert on the Atlanta Cyclorama, and is the go-to guy on the Atlanta History Center's acclaimed Civil War collections. Gould Hagler has similarly emerged as the authority on Georgia's Confederate monuments. *Audemus jura nostra defendere (We dare defend our rights)*, those stone inscriptions read, and no one knows this better than Gould.

Jack and Peggy Melton, publishers of *Civil War News*, took photographs at Jonesboro and Newnan when I so very much needed them, so I thank these shutterbugs extraordinaire.

Author Stephen Davis delights in showing visitors the lost traces of the fighting around Atlanta, which have largely been lost to urban sprawl. (ahc)

Dan Davis also assisted with photography; my thanks go to him, as well.

Finally, my gratitude to Ted Savas, owner and managing director of Savas Beatie publishing, not only for his faith in and encouragement for *mea opera civilis belli (my Civil War work)*, but also because he brings such a sane perspective to all the stuff we writers do. Witness how he signed himself for a recent book review: "The recovering attorney and widely published author appreciates red wine, good cigars, expensive gin, wreck driving and Mozart. A classically trained pianist, he plays bass (Rickenbackers only) in the hard rock band Arminius." To paraphrase Bob Dylan ("Well I might look like a Robert Ford, but I feel just like a Jesse James"): I may be a Steve Davis, but I wish I were a Ted Savas.

Stephen Davis
Marietta, Georgia
January 2017

PHOTO CREDITS:
Atltanta History Center (ahc); Dan Davis (dd); Gould Hagler (gh); *Harper's Weekly* (hw); Historical Marker Database (hmdd); Historical Publications, LLC (hp); Library of Congress (loc); Chris Mackowski (cm); Nash Farm (nf); *Photographic History of the Civil War* (phcw); Wikipedia Commons (wc)

For the Emerging Civil War Series

Theodore P. Savas, *publisher*
Chris Mackowski, *series editor*
Kristopher D. White, *chief historian*
Sarah Keeney, *editorial consultant*

Maps by Hal Jespersen
Historical content editing by Daniel T. Davis
Design and layout by H. R. Gordon
Publication supervision by Chris Mackowski

"Let us give these southern fellows all the fighting they want and when they are tired we can tell them we are just warming to the work."
— *Sherman to Grant, August 7, 1864*

John Bell Hood at Gaines's Mill

PROLOGUE

MAY 1862

In late spring of 1862, Confederate Brig. Gen. John Bell Hood was a promising brigade commander in Gen. Robert E. Lee's Army of Northern Virginia. All of 31 years old, he had risen in rank from first lieutenant, distinguishing himself in a couple of small engagements. But like many Southern officers, he remained largely untested in battle.

That was about to change.

In early May '62, Maj. Gen. George B. McClellan's ponderous Union army crept toward Richmond from southeast Virginia, pushing Confederate forces back. After Gen. Joseph E. Johnston was wounded in battle, General Lee took command of the Army of Northern Virginia on June 1. Lee was determined to drive back McClellan's army, which had slowly advanced to within five miles of the Confederate capital. To assist, he brought Maj. Gen. Thomas J. "Stonewall" Jackson's troops from the Shenandoah Valley. On June 27, Lee planned an attack on Union Brig. Gen. Fitz John Porter's corps at Gaines's Mill north of the Chickahominy River.

Porter's infantry were deployed on high

On the afternoon of June 27, 1862, during the Seven Days Battles, Brig. Gen. John B. Hood led the Confederate charge across the Boatswain's Creek that broke the enemy line in the battle of Gaines's Mill. His success marked him in Lee's and Jackson's eyes as a talented officer likely destined for promotion. (dd)

Kentuckian John Bell Hood was thirty years old when he received his promotion as Confederate brigadier general. Because of his prewar service in Texas, Hood came to be called "the gallant Hood of Texas." (nps)

Maj. Gen. Thomas J. Jackson expressed admiration for Hood and his Texans after their triumphant charge at Gaines's Mill. "The men who carried this position were soldiers indeed," he later remarked. (loc)

ground to the east of marshy Boatswain's Creek. The Confederate assault began at 2:30 with the advance of Maj. Gen. A. P. Hill's division. Hill's troops faltered under hot enemy artillery fire. Next, the attack of Maj. Gen. Richard S. Ewell's division was also repulsed, as was that of Maj. Gen. James Longstreet's troops. Major General Daniel H. Hill's attack fared a bit better; his men overran a Yankee battery, but were pushed back by a counterattack.

With the afternoon passing away, Lee was getting worried. As dusk approached, he ordered one last assault along the whole line. Lee encountered Hood as he led his "Texas Brigade"—three regiments from the Lone Star State and one from Georgia—toward the battlefield. Lee pointed out the daunting challenges ahead: 800 yards to cross, the swampy creek bed, then up the rise against three lines of enemy infantry with artillery. "This must be done," Lee explained. "Can you break this line?"

Hood answered simply, "I will try."

Before ordering the charge, Hood addressed the men of the 4th Texas, his first regimental command. "Soldiers, I have come to fulfill a promise I made to you while colonel of your regiment," he declared. "I promised to lead you personally in the first great battle. The time has come, and I am here."

Then he gave the order to advance. On horseback he led his brigade down the slope. Nearing the creek, he dismounted and gave the command to fix bayonets and to press on at the double-quick. Hood led the charge up the ridge. The Confederates overran and broke the first Union line, pushing so closely that Federals in their second line could not get off good volleys. Hood's impetuous charge broke that line, too.

"We flew towards the breastworks, cleared them," recalled one Texan, "and slaughtered the retreating devils as they scampered up the hill toward their battery."

After aligning his troops for the final charge, Hood led them on. "Forward! Steady!" he shouted. "Charge right down on them, and drive them out with the bayonet!"

They did. Hood's attack broke Porter's last line and pursued the fleeing Yankees till daylight gave out. The Confederates captured 14 Northern cannon in their sweep of the battlefield.

Hood's magnificent performance won commendation from Stonewall Jackson himself: "The Fourth Texas, under the lead of General Hood, was the first to pierce these strongholds and seize the guns." Lee also paid compliment to "the brave Texans." Both Jackson and Lee marked Hood as an officer of promise. Future promotions would come, and greater glory still would be won.

And it all started with a frontal assault against strong enemy lines. Hood had begun to build his reputation as a fearless attacker.

The Summer of '64

CHAPTER ONE

In the summer of 1864, the American Civil War entered its third year. Since their opening defeat at Bull Run, Federal forces had won significant victories at Shiloh, Gettysburg, and elsewhere. They had captured Rebel armies at Fort Donelson and Vicksburg, and had seized control of the Mississippi River. They had conquered and were occupying much Southern territory, including three state capitals.

Despite these Northern triumphs, however, the end of the war was nowhere in sight. The Confederate government and much of the Southern citizenry remained determined in their fight for national independence. That spring, Robert E. Lee's Army of Northern Virginia seemed to be holding Grant's forces at bay outside Richmond and Petersburg, and Confederate troops had defeated Union expeditions in Virginia's Shenandoah Valley and Louisiana's Red River.

On the other hand, in Georgia, Union Maj. Gen. William T. Sherman's forces had fought and maneuvered their way through north Georgia and seemed to be on the verge of capturing Atlanta. In mid-July, when Confederate Gen. Joseph E. Johnston, commanding the Army

After he withdrew his army across the Chattahoochee River, July 9-10, Confederate Gen. Joseph E. Johnston pitched his headquarters at the home of Dexter Niles, in the northwest suburbs of Atlanta. It was here on the evening of July 17 that Johnston received the telegram from Richmond relieving him from command of the Army of Tennessee. The house was destroyed in the summer of 1864, possibly by Northern cannon fire. The site, today at 1042 Marietta Street, is marked by a stack of cannonballs and a marker placed in 1920 by the Atlanta Chapter, United Daughters of the Confederacy. (ahc)

This marker stands on the grounds of the Carter Presidential Center and Library in east Atlanta. By the time Gen. John B. Hood took command of the Confederate Army of Tennessee, Union forces were just a few miles outside of the city. The Confederate administration in Richmond knew the odds were against Hood. "It may yet be practicable," telegraphed Secretary of War James A. Seddon, "to find or make an opportunity of equal encounter." Hood heeded Seddon's advice; his battles to save Atlanta would soon ensue. (ahc)

of Tennessee, could not provide a plan for saving the city or defeating Sherman, President Jefferson Davis relieved him of command. To succeed him the government promoted Lt. Gen. John B. Hood, then leading an infantry corps in Johnston's army. Confederate States Secretary of War James A. Seddon spelled out to Hood his task: find a way to defeat the enemy in battle, send his cavalry to cut Sherman's railroad supply line—do anything he could, in other words, to save Atlanta.

Both sides considered the city important. Reflecting this, Confederate engineers had begun constructing a fortified perimeter around the city more than a year before Sherman approached it. Yet by the time he did, Atlanta's was an importance largely in terms of psychology and morale. The city had been a vital manufacturing center, but much of its heavy machinery had been transported elsewhere as the Yankees approached. It was also a key railroad junction, but Sherman's forces had cut all but one railroad leading into the city (that one, leading south to Macon, supplied Hood's army). Thus Atlanta had become largely symbolic. For Jefferson Davis, holding onto Atlanta would demonstrate Confederate resilience and determination.

For Davis's Northern counterpart, Abraham Lincoln, the capture of Atlanta would have immense political impact. 1864 was a presidential election year in the United States, and Lincoln worried that the Northern people, tired of the war, might vote him out of office. If Sherman could capture Atlanta before the election in November, on the other hand, Lincoln could tell the people he was winning the war. His re-election prospects would be that much stronger.

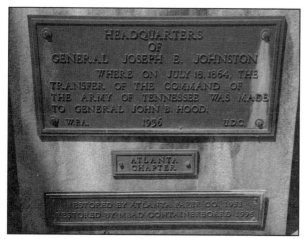

Johnston was studying maps with his chief engineer at the Niles house on July 17 when a telegram arrived. "As you have failed to arrest the advance of the enemy to the vicinity of Atlanta," it read, "and express no confidence that you can defeat or repel him, you are hereby relieved from the command of the Army and Department of Tennessee." John B. Hood, promoted to the rank of full general, succeeded Johnston the next day. (ahc)

Southerners realized this, too. In July 1864, the Northern Democratic Party had increasingly come to oppose the war; a number of its key leaders called for an armistice to stop the killing. If a Northern "peace Democrat" were nominated in August and elected in

Welcome to the urban landscape of Civil War remembrance. Here, on Marietta Street in northwest Atlanta, the U.D.C. monument set in 1920 to mark the site of Johnston's headquarters fortunately remains. To its right in this view is a flagpole; the Confederate banner which once waved aloft is, of course, long gone. Gone, too, is the state historical marker placed here in the mid-1950s explaining the role of the Dexter Niles house; a bent metal post is all that stands today. (ahc)

November, Confederates believed—at least hoped—that the new administration might call for a cease-fire. In that case, the secession of the Southern states from the Union would become a de facto reality. In short, a number of people in the Confederacy believed they could win their independence if Lincoln were denied a major battlefield victory—if Robert E. Lee kept Ulysses S. Grant out of Richmond and if John B. Hood kept William T. Sherman out of Atlanta.

Born in southern Ohio in 1822, Hiram Ulysses Grant won appointment to West Point in 1839 as Ulysses Simpson (his mother's maiden name) Grant. After service in the army, 1843-54, Grant resigned to pursue a series of unsuccessful callings. He was appointed colonel of an Illinois regiment in June 1861. His spectacular capture of Rebel forts guarding the Tennessee and Cumberland Rivers in February 1862 began a brilliant war record that led to Northern victories at Shiloh, Vicksburg, and Chattanooga. In March 1864, Abraham Lincoln gave him command of all Union forces, with the rank of lieutenant general. Grant was put in charge of directing strategy for all Federal armies in the spring campaign, but his focus would be on Robert E. Lee's Rebel army in Virginia. (loc)

Like Grant, William T. Sherman went to West Point and spent several years (1840-53) in the army before resigning. Like Grant, before the war he tried his luck at a few different vocations. With the outbreak, he won a colonel's commission and in the fall of 1861 assumed a post in Kentucky. There he apparently suffered a mental breakdown and was sent home. Returned to service, he fought under Grant at Shiloh and subsequently in the Vicksburg Campaign and at Chattanooga. When Lincoln summoned Grant east in early 1864 as U. S. general in chief, Sherman replaced him as commander of the Military Division of the Mississippi.

Such a rise would have been impossible without Grant's help. Sherman once quipped about this: "General Grant is a great general. I know him well. He stood by me when I was crazy and I stood by him when he was drunk; and now, sir, we stand by each other always." (loc)

In the spring of 1864, most Southerners placed their hopes for victory on Gen. Robert E. Lee and his Army of Northern Virginia. If Lee could successfully defend Richmond and Joe Johnston could thwart Sherman's advance on Atlanta, the Confederacy might persuade a war-weary North to agree to an armistice, which might recognize the Southern states' secession.

Professor James G. Randall summarized the situation in his *Civil War and Reconstruction* (1937): "The Mississippi River was in Union hands; Tennessee, West Virginia, and Virginia north of the Rapidan were held by Federal forces; most of the coast fortresses along the Atlantic and the Gulf were in Northern control; Louisiana was largely in Union occupation. On the other hand the vast bulk of the Confederacy was still unshaken; Southern arms held the rich Shenandoah Valley; and two powerful armies—Lee's in Virginia and Johnston's in northwestern Georgia—were ready to do battle against the Yankee invader." (loc)

Before the Civil War, Joseph E. Johnston was one of the brightest stars of the United States Army. Born in February 1807 (a month after Robert E. Lee) in Virginia, he was a classmate of Lee's at West Point. In the old army, he served with distinction in the Mexican War. At the time of Fort Sumter, he actually outranked Lee, having risen to brigadier general heading the Quartermaster Department in Washington (Lee was a colonel in the field). In the early months of the Confederacy, Johnston got a command leading troops in the Shenandoah Valley while Lee got a desk job in Richmond.

After Manassas, however, Johnston fell afoul of President Jefferson Davis. He quarreled over the issue of rank (in the appointment of generals, Lee got seniority). Commanding C. S. forces in northern Virginia in March 1862, he abandoned Centreville and tons of supplies without informing the administration. As McClellan advanced up the Peninsula, Johnston fell back to the capital before finally offering battle in late May at Seven Pines. There Johnston was seriously wounded. He relinquished command of the Army of Northern Virginia to Lee and never got it back.

After his return to duty, Johnston continued to disappoint President Davis, failing to aggressively support John C. Pemberton's besieged army at Vicksburg. Nevertheless, after Braxton Bragg's disaster at Missionary Ridge in November 1863, Davis gave Johnston one more chance as commander of the Army of Tennessee.

The president and the Southern people were in for more disappointment when Johnston, from early May to mid-July 1864, fell back through north Georgia, allowing Sherman to bring his armies to the very gates of Atlanta. The retreating cost Johnston his job. (loc)

Hood Takes Command

CHAPTER TWO

In a telegram to Hood on July 17, Secretary Seddon acknowledged the steep odds the new army commander faced. "Position, numbers and morale are now with the enemy," Seddon wrote, and indeed they were. After Sherman managed to get a bridgehead on the south bank of the Chattahoochee and forced the Confederates to retreat across the river, Johnston positioned his army several miles to its south. The Southerners dug a seven- or eight-mile line of entrenchments south of Peachtree Creek, a stream running from east to west into the Chattahoochee. The line ran just two miles from the city limits.

Johnston did nothing to contest the Federals' crossing; indeed, he gave Sherman a full week to get his troops to the south bank. On July 17, the day Johnston was relieved, Sherman had his infantry marching toward Atlanta. By the end of the day, Yankees were within five miles of the city's suburbs.

When Hood assumed command on July 18, his army occupied the outer defense line, which Johnston and his chief engineer, Lt. Col.

In Johnston's retreat through north Georgia, May-July, a few bright spots occurred. Several times Sherman's infantry attacked prepared Confederate positions and were decisively repulsed. One of these Confederate victories occurred on May 27 at Pickett's Mill, shown here in a modern view of the Georgia state-owned battlefield park.
(dd)

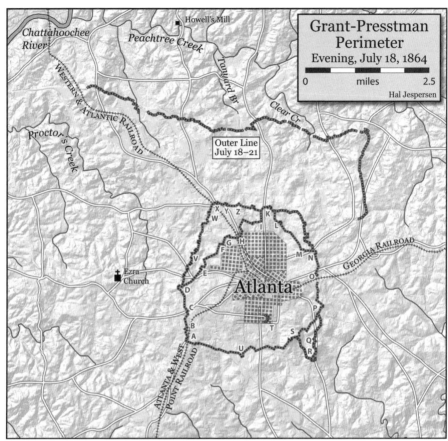

GRANT-PRESSTMAN PERIMETER—Capt. Lemuel Grant had laid out the fortifications surrounding Atlanta well before Sherman's approach. Confederates hurried to complete northwest and northeast salients in the first days of General Hood's accession to command. General Johnston and his engineer, Lt. Col. Stephen Presstman, were planning an outer line south of Peachtree Creek on the night of July 17, when he was relieved. The letters within the map represent the location of Confederate artillery positions.

Stephen Presstman, had laid out about the time he was relieved. Hood set his men to working hard to strengthen it, along with the main perimeter of defenses around the city. These fortifications were formidable. A continuous 10-and-a-half-mile circle of entrenchments ringed the city, averaging a mile and a half from the city's edges. To the northwest and northeast, additional works were constructed, so the perimeter eventually ran 12 miles. It included two dozen artillery forts, and *abatis, chevaux-de-frise* and palisades were set out in front to impede an enemy infantry assault. For forests cut down to provide wood for trench revetments and to clear fields of fire, the C. S. government reimbursed the property owners.

The extensive and formidable defenses of Atlanta were the only factor helping Hood and his army. Otherwise Sherman had the edge. Numbers, as Seddon had stated, especially favored the Federals. In mid-July, Sherman's army invading Georgia really amounted to an army *group*, consisting of three separate armies.

Largest of them was the army of the Cumberland, commanded by Maj. Gen. George H. Thomas. Consisting of three big corps—the IV, XIV and XX—Thomas's army on June 30 numbered 46,813 infantry officers and men.

Major General James B. McPherson's Army of the Tennessee had previously been Sherman's own command before Sherman had been promoted to lead the Military Division of the Mississippi after Grant was called to Virginia. McPherson's three corps—the XV, XVI and XVII—counted 29,266 infantry on the last day of June.

Smallest contingent of the army group was Maj. Gen. John M. Schofield's "Army of the Ohio," which was really only a single infantry corps—the XXIII—with all of two divisions, 12,007 men.

Sherman's cavalry was organized in four divisions under Kenner Garrard, Edward McCook, Judson Kilpatrick, and George Stoneman. They totaled 12,039 sabers at the start of July. The artillery had 254 guns at the start of the campaign. By this time, the number of men serving them totaled 5,945. Thus Sherman's army group counted 106,070 officers and men as of June 30.

As he took command of the Army of Tennessee in mid-July 1864, John B. Hood faced the challenge of inexperienced corps commanders. After the death of Lt. Gen. Leonidas Polk on June 14, Maj. Gen. William W. Loring took over for a few weeks. But on July 7, Maj. Gen. Alexander Peter Stewart, shown here, succeeded to command of Polk's corps. His promotion to lieutenant general was ratified by President Davis on June 23, effective June 2. Stewart had risen through the Army of Tennessee as a dependable brigade and division commander. When Hood succeeded Joe Johnston on July 18, "Old Straight"—as Stewart was called—had been a corps leader for less than two weeks. (loc)

Born to a prosperous Nashville family in 1820, Benjamin Franklin Cheatham won appointment as colonel of a Tennessee regiment in the Mexican War. A planter in the 1850s, Cheatham was given a military post by Tennessee Governor Isham Harris. Despite a lack of formal soldier's training, he received a Confederate brigadier's rank in July 1861. He fought at Belmont, Missouri, November 1861, and was promoted to major general in March 1862. Cheatham led a division at Shiloh, Perryville, and Murfreesboro. After service at Chickamauga and Missionary Ridge, Cheatham commanded his division of Tennesseans in Johnston's army, fighting well in the battles of the Atlanta Campaign. When Hood took army command in July, he appointed Frank Cheatham as commander of his corps. (loc)

The closest return for Johnston's army is dated July 10. It showed 43,073 infantry officers and men present for duty; 12,379 cavalrymen; and 3,744 in the artillery—totaling 59,196. That meant Johnston had about 56 percent of Sherman's strength. Numerically, the odds against the Confederates were roughly six-to-10.

Morale also favored the Federals. When they reached the Chattahoochee, Sherman had pushed his forces a hundred miles from Chattanooga. Sherman and Johnston had fought in several battles: at Resaca, May 14-15, in the Pickett's Mill/New Hope Church/Dallas area, May 25-28, and at Kennesaw Mountain, June 27, with heavy skirmishes approaching small battles elsewhere. By this time in the war, troops on the defensive always dug in and fortified, so whoever did the attacking was repulsed. Yet after every battle, Sherman had been able to swing McPherson or Schofield around Johnston's flank, forcing Johnston to retreat to yet another position farther to the rear. In withdrawing across the Chattahoochee during the night of July 9-10, Johnston had given up nine different positions since leaving Rocky Face Ridge two months earlier.

Sherman's successes infused his officers and men with buoyant spirit. "Our men are hopeful and cheerful and speak of the summer campaign as being the last," Illinois Sgt. Maj. Lyman Widney wrote home. "They are confident of Grant's success and, too, of our own success, regarded as so certain as that the sun will rise tomorrow morning."

Conversely, while many Confederates remained confident, Johnston's retreating understandably weakened the morale of some of his men. "I don't like giving up so much territory," Capt. Wallace Howard of the 63rd

It is ironic that we owe most photographs of Confederate fortifications surrounding Atlanta to a Northern photographer, George Barnard. A contract cameraman for the Union army, Barnard was summoned to Atlanta by Sherman's chief engineer, Capt. Orlando Poe, shortly after the Federals occupied the city. For the next two months, Barnard shot such images as this, the Rebel Fort Hood near the Western & Atlantic Railroad in the defenses northwest of the city. Note the photographer's developing tent beyond the chevaux-de-frise, in front of the earthen parapet. (loc)

Georgia told another officer as he watched the army march across the Chattahoochee. "It looks to me like the beginning of the end, as though we were going right straight down to the Gulf of Mexico." On July 10, with the army on the south river bank, Capt. W. L. Trask, a Confederate staff officer, recorded in his diary, "we feel much dejected and low spirited at our prospects."

The Confederate retreat to the outskirts of the city scared many Atlantans, who gathered up their belongings as they could, secured transport, and fled. "Everybody seems to be hurrying off," a reporter for the *Mobile News* observed; "every train of cars is loaded to its utmost capacity."

For his part, Hood could only evince optimism to his troops. "I look with confidence to your patriotism," he announced to the army when he took command from Johnston. All knew, however, they faced a most difficult task keeping Sherman out of Atlanta.

The Union commander already had his plan in mind. He knew from spy reports that Atlanta was strongly fortified, and he knew he would not send his infantry charging against the Rebel works. "I was willing to meet the enemy in

A native of Ohio, James McPherson graduated first in his West Point class of 1853. After duty in the prewar engineers, he entered the Union army as lieutenant, and in the Henry-Donelson campaign, elevated to lieutenant colonel, served as Ulysses Grant's chief engineer. He became brigadier in August 1862 and major general several months later. In Grant's Vicksburg campaign he led the XVII Corps, winning praise from Major General Sherman. When Sherman was bumped up to lead the Military Division of the Mississippi before the opening of the Atlanta Campaign, McPherson succeeded him in command of the Army of the Tennessee. (loc)

Born into a planter family in southeast Georgia in 1815, William J. Hardee attended the U. S. Military Academy and embarked on a lifelong military career. He won distinction in the Mexican War and fame as author of Hardee's Tactics (1855), a manual for army officers. When Georgia seceded, Hardee resigned his commission as a lieutenant colonel. Appointed Confederate brigadier in June 1861, Hardee was sent west, commanding troops under Albert Sidney Johnston. Promoted to major general, he fought at Shiloh and led half of Braxton Bragg's infantry during the Confederate raid into Kentucky, October 1862. That month, he was promoted lieutenant general and took command of an infantry corps in the Army of Tennessee. He would hold that position another two years, earning reputation for reliability if not brilliance. (loc)

Without military training, Illinois-born John A. Logan volunteered for service in the Mexican War. When the Civil War began, as a Democratic congressman and political leader, he recruited an Illinois infantry regiment, of which he became colonel. He served under Grant at Fort Donelson, after which he was promoted to brigadier general. A major generalship followed a year later. "Black Jack," as he was called, led a division in the Vicksburg campaign and, by the start of the Atlanta Campaign, had been placed in command of the Union XV Corps. (loc)

the open country," he later explained, "but not behind well-constructed parapets." Nor did he have the manpower to completely surround the Rebels in their works. Sherman determined to force Hood from Atlanta by cutting the several railroads that brought in food and supplies for Hood's army while Federal forces conducted something of a semi-siege.

Sherman accordingly ordered his three

armies to approach Atlanta from the north and east, swinging far enough around so as to reach and tear up the Georgia Railroad running toward Augusta. Once that line was rendered useless to the Rebels, Sherman planned to move against the other railway lines serving them.

Hood could not protect all the railroads, especially when the Yankees could cut them at any point. On July 18, Union Brig. Gen. Kenner Garrard's cavalry and some of McPherson's infantry reached the Georgia Railroad 13 miles east of Atlanta and began wrecking it as they moved westward toward the city. North of Atlanta, Thomas approached Peachtree Creek; Schofield pushed toward the city from the northeast, between the two other armies.

On the 18th, Hood got more bad news: enemy cavalry had cut the railroad connecting Atlanta with Montgomery. Major General Lovell H. Rousseau had led 2,700 Northern horsemen out of north Alabama and on July 17 reached the Montgomery & West Point Railroad near Auburn. Riding east along the line, they destroyed two dozen miles of track before riding off to join Sherman's forces at Atlanta. The damage was not repaired till late August. For all intents, Atlanta's connection to Montgomery was cut. For the rest of the campaign Hood could only depend on the Macon & Western Railroad for the supplies needed by his men and animals.

. . . And needed by the civilians still in the city, too, of whom thousands remained. At the start of the year, Atlanta's population had numbered about 20,000. Many of these had fled upon the Yankees' approach, especially after Johnston's army retreated across the Chattahoochee. Unless they had gardens or livestock, these people needed food, too, and were thus also dependent upon the Macon railroad.

A native Kentuckian, Lovell H. Rousseau moved to Indiana where he practiced law in the 1840s. He served creditably in Mexico and was elected to the state legislature. Returning to Kentucky, with the outbreak of hostilities he resigned his seat in the state senate to raise troops for the Union. He rose to brigadier's rank, leading a brigade at Shiloh and a division at Perryville and Stones River. From November 1863 to the end of the war, he commanded the Union District of Tennessee at Nashville. Despite his lack of cavalry experience, in the summer of 1864 he was ordered by Sherman to organize a raid into Alabama against enemy railroads. Rousseau's raid, July 10-22, has been called "one of the most successful Federal cavalry operations of the Civil War." (loc)

More immediately, Hood had to contend with the enemy columns closing in on Atlanta. On July 19, Thomas's infantry started laying makeshift bridges across the deep-ravined Peachtree Creek at several points as close as one mile north of the Confederates' outer line. On McPherson's front, Maj. Gen. John A. Logan's XV Corps marched to Decatur, six miles east of Atlanta.

Sherman called for his infantry to destroy more of the Augusta railroad's track and prescribed how he wanted it done. "Pile the ties into shape for a bonfire," the orders read, "put the rails across, and when red hot, in the middle let a man at each end twist the bar so that its surface become spiral." All this was to keep the enemy from readily repairing their road. "Officers should be directed," Sherman lectured, "that bars simply bent may be used again, but if when red hot they are twisted out of line they cannot be used again."

*   *   *

Hood spent his first full day of command, July 19, attending to administrative matters, such as appointing a replacement to lead his old corps. He chose Maj. Gen. Benjamin Franklin Cheatham, though the assignment was intended only as temporary. Elevating Cheatham from division to corps command left an opening for the head of Cheatham's division: Brig. Gen. George E. Maney was named to fill it, effective July 19.

On the front lines, Confederates tried to impede the enemy's approach. After Federals got across Peachtree Creek that afternoon, an Arkansas brigade charged and tried, unsuccessfully, to drive them back over the stream. Wheeler's cavalry contested

McPherson's advance from Decatur, but the Southern horsemen, greatly outnumbered, could barely slow the Yankees down.

On the morning of July 19, Sherman learned of the command change in the Army of Tennessee. With the Federals' approach and the hurried exodus of many citizens, most of the city's newspapers had also fled. Still staying, at least for a few days more, was the Atlanta *Appeal,* originally from Memphis. A spy picked up its issue announcing the change in the city and took it to Union lines. Sherman thus learned of Hood's promotion. John Schofield, who had been Hood's classmate at West Point, advised his commander of what the news meant: there would be fighting ahead.

Schofield was right. Secretary Seddon had urged Hood to seek opportunity to deliver an attacking battle on anything approaching equal terms, and Hood on the 19th began to see just such an opportunity. Thomas's army was the largest in Sherman's army group, but in the process of crossing Peachtree Creek, it would be divided and vulnerable to attack. Even if the enemy infantry deployed on the south creek bank before he could launch his assault, Hood reasoned that they would not have had time to fortify much, if at all. Moreover, Schofield's army was not in immediate supporting distance. To close the gap, Thomas had sent Howard and two divisions off to the southeast, but a two-mile gap still existed between them and the left of Thomas's line. This would disappear when Sherman drew his three armies in closer to Atlanta, forming them into a unified front. Clearly the time to strike was now.

Joe Johnston later claimed that the idea of attacking Thomas at Peachtree Creek was *his*, and that before he left the army he had

Graduate of West Point (1853), John McAllister Schofield was teaching physics at Washington University in St. Louis when war broke out. Accepting commission in Missouri's Union forces, Schofield fought under Nathaniel Lyon at Springfield/Wilson's Creek. Made brigadier in November 1861 and major general a year later, he commanded the Department of Missouri. At the start of the Atlanta Campaign, he led the Army of the Ohio—consisting of just the XXIII Corps—which would be the smallest of Sherman's three armies. (loc)

James Alexander Seddon was the quintessential Virginia aristocrat. Born on a plantation and schooled at the University of Virginia, Seddon became an attorney, legislator, and planter before the war. In the fall of 1862, he accepted the position of Secretary of War in Jefferson Davis's Cabinet. He served in this capacity longer than any of the Confederacy's other five war secretaries, in large part because of his ability to get along with the president. (wc)

explained his plan to Hood. The two generals, writing their memoirs in the 1870s, clashed over this point. "In transferring the command to General Hood I explained my plans to him," Johnston wrote in his *Narrative* (1874); "I expected an opportunity to engage the enemy on terms of advantage while they were divided in crossing Peach-Tree Creek." Hood, on the other hand, claimed in his *Advance and Retreat* (1880) that "the Federal commander had committed a serious blunder in separating his corps, or Armies by such distance as to allow me to concentrate the main body of our Army upon his right wing." It was Wheeler's intelligence of the enemy's dispositions, Hood contended, that led to his formulation of the battle plan, not anything Johnston allegedly told him.

Historians continue to take sides as to who should be credited with the plan to attack Thomas at Peachtree Creek. After the war, a Confederate congressman, George Vest of Missouri, claimed that he was visiting General Johnston when news came in that the Federals were crossing the creek. "Gentlemen, the time has come to strike," Johnston allegedly declared; "Sherman has cut his army into three pieces and I believe now by rapid movements, I can whip him in detail." The problem with the Vest recollection, though, is that its timing is wrong. By the time George Thomas's infantry were crossing Peachtree Creek on July 19, Joe Johnston had already been relieved of command.

Another argument in favor of Johnston's plan-authorship is similarly flawed. Confederate Sgt. T. G. Dabney contended after the war that, on the afternoon of July 16, "a circular battle order was promulgated among the troops from General Johnston, which stated that the favorable opportunity had arrived for striking the enemy." Johnston purportedly announced, "We would advance at daylight next morning and beat him." The afternoon of July 16 was the very time Joe Johnston was telling authorities in Richmond that his "plan of operations must . . . depend upon that of the enemy. It is mainly to watch for an opportunity to fight to advantage." If Johnston planned to attack the enemy the next morning, he most certainly should have told his superiors.

But the operative word is *if.* After the war, Judah P. Benjamin recounted the reason that, in the Confederate Cabinet meeting of mid-July 1864, he had voted to relieve Johnston of army command: "his nervous dread of <u>losing a battle</u> would prevent at all times his ability to cope with an enemy of nearly equal strength." There is no reason to believe that before Atlanta, with the fate of the city—indeed possibly the entire Confederate cause—at stake, Joseph E. Johnston would have successfully managed to swallow "his nervous dread of <u>losing a battle</u>."

Incidentally, just as we don't know what Joseph E. Johnston would have done had he been retained in command, neither do we know what Lt. Gen. William J. Hardee would have done if *he* had been appointed to succeed Johnston. Hardee had been in charge of a corps in the Army of Tennessee since October 1862, when he was promoted to lieutenant general. John Bell Hood had been a corps commander for all of six months when he was elevated over Hardee's head to army command. How Hood's supersedure of Hardee may have affected the latter's performance in the arduous days ahead we will have occasion to consider.

Virginian George Henry Thomas suffered estrangement from his sisters when he declared for the Union in 1861. West Pointer, artilleryman in the old army, Seminole and Mexican War veteran, Thomas was commissioned brigadier general in August 1861. He won an early Northern victory at Mill Springs, Kentucky, in January 1862. Major general in the western Federal armies, his shining moment was taking the stand at Chickamauga, September 20, 1863, which saved William S. Rosecrans's army from total disaster after Rebels broke its lines. He succeeded Rosecrans a month later in command of the Army of the Cumberland—the position he would exercise throughout the Atlanta Campaign. (loc)

The Battle of Peachtree Creek

CHAPTER THREE

Having determined to attack Thomas's Army of the Cumberland, Hood could waste no time, so he determined to launch his battle the very next day. On the night of July 19, he called together his three corps commanders— Lt. Gens. William Hardee and Peter Stewart, and Maj. Gen. Frank Cheatham—to his headquarters, a house on Peachtree Street just north of the city limits. Wheeler and Smith were there, too. He explained the overall idea and the role of each officer in it.

Cheatham was to help Wheeler's cavalry and Maj. Gen. Gustavus W. Smith's Georgia Militia hold McPherson's army from getting closer to the city. McPherson was, at the time, two-and-a-half miles to the east. The length of the outer defense line increased the Southerners' difficulties. Northeast of the city, the line angled south but ended a mile north of the Georgia Railroad, which was McPherson's march route. The works would have to be extended if the Confederates stood a chance of blocking McPherson's further advance.

Meanwhile, Hardee's and Stewart's corps

On July 19, Thomas's Army of the Cumberland started crossing Peachtree Creek, a deep-ravined stream flowing north of Atlanta. Confederates delayed their advance and burned bridges, but with makeshift foot-crossings all nine of Thomas's infantry divisions were on the south bank of the creek by noon of July 20. (dd)

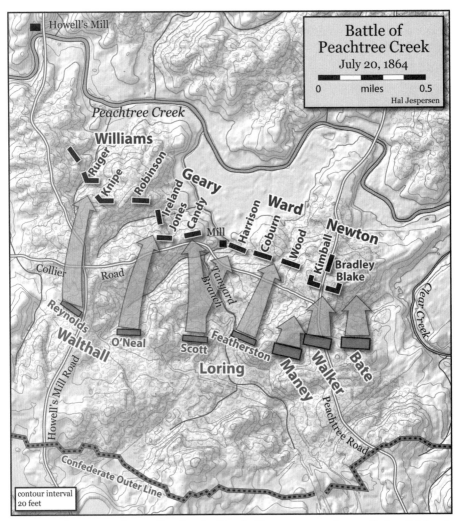

BATTLE OF PEACHTREE CREEK—Hood's attacking battle encompassed assaults by division in echelon from the Confederate right. Begun around 4 p.m. on July 20, the fighting had sputtered out with Walthall's division by sundown.

were to attack Thomas beginning at 1 p.m. the next day. It would be an echelon attack by division from the right, similar in plan to Lee's for July 2 at Gettysburg. Six divisions were to take part, advancing east to west one after another. The order began with Hardee's three divisions, commanded by Maj. Gens. William B. Bate, William H. T. Walker, and George B. Maney, who had taken charge of Cheatham's division. Then the advance would be taken up by Stewart's Corps: Maj. Gens. William W. Loring's, Edward C. Walthall's, and Samuel G. French's divisions.

Students of the battle have not puzzled over why Hood and Hardee held back Maj. Gen. Patrick R. Cleburne's division, arguably the best in the army, and kept it in reserve. Logic would explain that Hardee was saving it to press success, if the assault were successful, and start rolling up the enemy line. Possibly less logical might be the hypothesis that Hardee, the aggrieved corps commander passed over for army command, was deliberately holding out his best division from Hood's first attack.

Hood knew the Yankees had gotten across Peachtree Creek, but could not as yet ascertain their strength. Nevertheless, he announced the objective: "everything on our side of the creek to be taken at all hazards." He went around the room and asked if all knew their roles in the plan. All said yes. Later, Stewart put his understanding this way: "the plan was . . . to attack the enemy, drive him back to the creek, and then press down the creek to the left. Should the enemy be found intrenched his works were to be carried, everything on our side of the creek was to be taken."

*   *   *

Battle is a highly fluid situation, it is said, and Hood's need to adapt to the situation's fluidity began on the morning of July 20, even before the Confederate attack on Thomas's army was to begin. Around 10 a.m., Wheeler sent worried word to headquarters that McPherson was marching hard on the city and that the Confederate cavalry was being pushed back. Hood sent him another 1,000 horsemen under Maj. Gen. William H. "Red" Jackson.

This George Barnard photograph, taken several months after the engagement fought on July 20, is the only known camera view of the battlefield of Peachtree Creek. It looks north from today's Collier Road toward the Union lines in the area assailed by Brig. Gen. Winfield S. Featherston's brigade. The graves in the foreground are those of Union soldiers; their headboards were placed by comrades. After the war, the federal government arranged for the remains of these dead to be reinterred in the U. S. National Cemetery at Marietta, north of Atlanta. (loc)

Hood also ordered infantry to the rescue by shifting his entire line to the right. All three corps were deployed that morning in the outer defense line south of Peachtree Creek. Hood instructed Cheatham, on the right, to march a mile or so farther south to reach the Georgia Railroad and block the enemy's route. The rest of the army was to shift right—Hood called it "a division front." Frank Cheatham, in his new corps role, unfortunately mismanaged the maneuver. It ended up taking three or four hours, throwing Hood's 1 p.m. assault badly off schedule.

Even if the Confederates had attacked as planned, they would have found all of Thomas's seven available divisions already across Peachtree Creek, deployed south of it. Off to the west, closest to the Chattahoochee, was Maj. Gen. John M. Palmer's XIV Corps. Palmer believed the Rebels might attack that day, so he directed his troops to start digging in.

Joe Hooker, commanding the XX Corps, disagreed and issued no order for entrenching that afternoon. "On this day, everyone from our Corps Commander to private soldier," recorded Sgt. Rice C. Bull of the 123rd New York in his diary, "seemed certain that the enemy would make no stand until behind the entrenchments at Atlanta"—meaning the main defensive perimeter, not the outer line of trenches. Sergeant Bull noticed the officers not only issued no orders for entrenching, but they did not even send forth their skirmish lines as far forward as they usually did.

With the Confederate "division front" shift taking too long, Hardee around 3:15 p.m. began to chafe, and ordered his infantry to launch the attack. No reconnaissance had been allowed beforehand, so when Bate's division advanced into the woods and thickets ahead of them, they found no enemy in their front. The Southerners had marched into that two-mile gap in Thomas's line. After flailing around in no-man's land and coming under artillery fire, Bate's troops began to fall back to their jump-off position.

Next, it was Walker's turn. Because of the line-gap, Walker's rightmost brigade never really got into the fight. But the rest of the charging division faced tough resistance. The Federals—Brig. Gen. John Newton's division of the IV Corps—occupied high ground astride Peachtree

Col. Benjamin Harrison commanded a brigade of Midwesterners in Brig. Gen. William T. Ward's 3rd division, Hooker's XX Corps at Peachtree Creek. Initially hard pressed, Harrison's troops counterattacked and drove back the Rebels. "The long distance the enemy charged on the double-quick," Harrison reported, had tired the enemy in their advance. "I could observe many of his men lying down and a few even turning back, while the officers, with their drawn swords, were trying to steady their lines and push them forward." After the war, Harrison rose in Indiana politics, serving in the U. S. Senate, 1881-87. In 1888 he was elected U. S. president, one of five ex-Union officers to occupy the White House after the Civil War. (loc)

The 1944 monument on the site of the battle of Peachtree Creek notes that it was "the first of the four conflicts for the possession of Atlanta." The Atlanta Historical Society dedicators were thinking of Peachtree Creek (July 20), Atlanta (July 22), Ezra Church (July 28) and Jonesboro (August 31-September 1). Sherman's semi-siege of Atlanta, though, which can be dated from July 20 to August 25, actually involved daily skirmishing and shelling between the opposing armies. Casualties from this incessant fighting, according to participants, amounted to losses usually incurred in a major battle. (dd)(dd)

A block south of the monument to American valor at Piedmont Hospital, this historical marker, placed in the 1950s, explains Confederates' activity in the two days before the battle of Peachtree Creek. Lt. Gen. William J. Hardee's infantry were posted in this area, guarding the creek crossings on July 18. Wheeler's cavalry contested the enemy advances north of the stream. On July 19 Union Brig. Gen. Thomas Wood's division of the IV Corps marched down Peachtree road and forced a crossing after Hardee's troops withdrew to the south bank and burned the bridge. (dd)

Road (today the ridge is called Cardiac Hill; Peachtree Road Race runners have to huff up it from the creek bed to the north). More, that afternoon, they had begun to throw up light works. Beyond that, Northern artillery and musketry took their toll. Thomas, from behind Newton's line, directed a destructive cannonfire. On the front line, Newton's men laid down fierce volleys. "We were evening up matters with June 27 (Kennesaw) in mind," remembered Lt. Ralsa Rice of the 125th Ohio.

Even though some of Confederate Brig. Gen. Clement H. Stevens's men got close to, and briefly topped, the enemy works, they were pushed back. Stevens was struck in the head and carried from the field; he died five days later. Walker's attack was spent. After fewer than 30 minutes, his troops fell back.

The performance of Maney's division, next to go in on Walker's left, was even lamer. In this sector, the Southerners advanced to maybe 60 yards of the Yankee line, exchanged fire for an hour or so, then traipsed back to their line. Historians have tried to be understanding of the Tennesseans' travails that afternoon. The day was hot, the men had to double-quick a half mile, and they got tired; they were charging uphill through brambles and brush; they didn't know exactly what was ahead of them; those who got close enough saw enemy works; they knew that Walker's troops had already been repulsed; the enemy fire was accurate and effective. Let's not forget that General Maney himself had never been tested as division commander.

The infantry of Stewart's corps fought much better that afternoon. A factor in their solid performance may have been the address that Stewart, riding in front of his troops, delivered before giving the order for the advance. Alabama Pvt. J. P. Cannon recalled hearing him announce, "We were going to assault the enemy in his works, and we must carry everything, allowing no obstacle to stop us; that the fate of Atlanta probably depended on the result of this battle."

Stewart's words seem to have mattered. Union Brig. Gen. John W. Geary, commanding the division about to be assailed, remarked that the advance of the Rebel troops in the field before his lines was "magnificent," and they "also seemed to rush forward with more than customary nerve and heartiness in the attack."

Brigadier General Winfield Scott Featherston's brigade of Mississippians was the first to go in. They crossed a field and climbed up a gentle ridge that has taken its informal name from the present-day Collier Road running along its east-west crest. Atop the Collier ridge were two Yankee regiments, which were driven back. Down the other slope and in line were two Federal brigades, which, alerted by the battle sounds, were unfortified but otherwise ready to meet the Rebels. They delivered volleys so heavy that Featherston's soldiers halted and fell back up the ridge, still under fire. The Northerners chased after them, pushed them over the ridge and back to their start-points. Featherston later reported half of his men—616 out of 1,200—had been killed, wounded, or had gone missing in the intense fighting.

The attack of Brig. Gen. Thomas Scott's brigade also made initial headway. On the right of the column, two Alabama regiments surged over Collier Road ridge, then down its slope into the fire of the brigade commanded by Col. Benjamin Harrison, the later United

Born in Pennsylvania in 1819, John White Geary pursued a number of callings: schoolteacher, store clerk, surveyor. Longtime militia service led to colonelcy of the 2nd Pennsylvania in the Mexican War. Afterward, he served as San Francisco's first mayor and territorial governor of Kansas during 1856-57, the height of pro- and anti-slavery turbulence in "Bleeding Kansas." Retiring to his Pennsylvania home, Geary organized the 28th Pennsylvania when civil war came, and was made its colonel in June 1861. Brigadier in spring 1862, he led a division in the XII Corps at Chancellorsville. In fall 1863, he went to the Tennessee theater. On October 28, in the battle of Wauhatchie near Chattanooga, Geary's division repulsed a Confederate attack, but the general's nineteen-year-old son Eddie, serving in the artillery, was shot in the head and died in his arms. After the XI and XII Corps were consolidated into the XX Corps in spring 1864, Geary commanded the 2nd division, XX Corps throughout the Atlanta Campaign. (loc)

Confederate Brig. Gen. Clement H. Stevens commanded a brigade in Maj. Gen. William H. T. Walker's division, attacking the enemy line north of today's Collier Road. The Southerners, according to one Union officer, advanced "with a rapidity and an absence of confusion I have never seen equaled." Two of Stevens's regiments overran the Yankee position before being driven back. Stevens was shot in the head during the afternoon's fighting. Surgeons removed the ball, and Stevens was transported to a hospital in Macon, south of Atlanta. There he died on July 25. (loc)

States president. The Alabamans were pushed back off the Collier Ridge and withdrew.

The assault of Scott's left enjoyed more success, but only at the start. The Confederates overwhelmed a New Jersey regiment that had been thrown out in advance; they captured its flag as the Federals were driven back to their line "in great confusion and disorder," lamented one Northern officer. The Southerners pressed ahead to the enemy line, overwhelmed part of it and captured three Napoleon guns. Colonel S. S. Ives of the 35th Alabama proudly reported that the Yankees "in their precipitous flight threw away their knapsacks, guns, and accoutrements." Then came the advance of Col. Edward O'Neal's brigade, the first of Walthall's division to enter the fight. O'Neal's assault caught part of the Yankee line in flank, putting several Northern regiments to flight. But Union artillery helped halt the Rebels, and reinforcements arrived to restore the line and retake the guns. Hooker himself rode about, encouraging his men. Against this new pressure, Scott ordered his troops to fall back.

After driving some of the Yankees and threatening to overrun their batteries, O'Neal's troops plunged into a ravine where they took flanking fire from both sides. "The brigade fell back," O'Neal reported, "not in very good order."

Brigadier General Daniel Reynolds's Arkansas brigade was the last of Walthall's divisions to join the engagement. The Confederates charged and got close to lines of Brig. Gen. Alpheus Williams's Union division. With O'Neal retired to their right and without support on their left, Reynolds's troops fell back after rather limited fighting; Reynolds counted six killed, 52 wounded, and nine missing.

By this time the sun was setting, so Brig. Gen.

William Quarles's brigade did not even launch a charge. The battle sputtered out before Stewart's leftmost division, French's, became engaged.

In Hood's first attacking battle, the Confederates had charged and overrun the Federal line in places, but by the end of the day had been repulsed. In terms of numbers, the opposing forces at Peachtree Creek were pretty evenly matched, about 20,000 men engaged on each side. Because they were primarily the attackers, the Southerners incurred higher casualties—but not that much higher. Federals lost 1,750-1,800 men, Confederates 2,300 to 2,500.

The relative closeness of the two numbers points out several aspects of the battle. First, the three divisions which Hardee committed to the battle either did not become engaged (Bate, who marched into the two-mile gap), or only partly

On Collier Road, across from Tanyard Creek Park, are two millstones from Andrew Jackson Collier's antebellum grist mill. The mill stood sixty feet downstream (to the north, as Tanyard Branch flows into Peachtree Creek). The area was the scene of heavy fighting in the Confederate attack on the afternoon of July 20. Collier heirs gave several acres for the City of Atlanta park in 1938. By that time, the abandoned wooden mill had rotted away. The Atlanta Historical Society dedicated these millstones in 1952. Years later, a metal cogwheel and shaft were found in creek silt and added to the millstone monument, as shown on the left. The plaques in the stone setting quote Union Gen. Jacob Cox: "Few battlefields of the war have been strewn so thickly with dead and wounded as they lay that evening around Collier's Mill." (dd)

The battle of July 20, having begun along Peachtree Road about 4 p.m., featured Confederate attacks by division in echelon from right (east) to left. By the time Brig. Gen. Daniel Reynolds's Arkansas brigade advanced, after five o'clock in this area (along Howell Mill Road), Hood's attack along much of the line had already been repulsed. (dd)

so (Walker) or halfheartedly (Maney). For some reason Hardee held back his best combat troops, Cleburne's division, which brings up the corps commander's performance in the battle. Lieutenant Thomas B. Mackall, nephew of Hood's chief of staff, Brig. Gen. William W. Mackall, also served at Hood's headquarters. The night of July 20 he entered in his journal, "Hardee does not think proper to attack eny's strong works." In other words, within hours of the battle's end, Hood's staff officers were already talking about Hardee's mediocre performance that day. Hood later claimed that Pat Cleburne told him that before the battle Hardee had warned his division commanders to look out for enemy breastworks ahead of them. This was a completely different message from what Stewart told his troops ("assault the enemy in his works . . . must carry everything . . . no obstacle to stop us"). Hood later telegraphed President Davis, "in the battle of July 20 we failed on account of General Hardee," and in his campaign report, Hood charged that "Hardee failed to push the attack."

Hardee vigorously defended himself, and the argument over his role at Peachtree Creek continues. Historians remain divided, although a recent chronicler of the battle, Robert Jenkins, has concluded that "it is fair to lay the loss at Peach Tree Creek at the feet of Hardee and two of his subordinates, Bate and Maney"—the latter because their two divisions failed to deliver strong assaults.

Dean of Atlanta Campaign scholars, the late Albert Castel, offers a shrewd observation about the battle: "where the Confederates had the advantage in strength [Hardee's corps], they did not fight well; and where they fought well [Stewart's corps], they were too weak."

But there were other factors in Hood's repulse, including the Yankees themselves. At some points in their line—*e.g.*, Newton's division—they had some manner of fortification. Artillery always helps defenders, and the Federals used theirs effectively; Thomas himself directed the fire of some of his guns.

The Southerners had their own problems, beginning with a long approach-distance on a hot afternoon. Hood's three-hour delay in launching his attack was not critical; all of Thomas's infantry had gotten across Peachtree Creek by noon. The echelon assault—here, from east to west—is intended to take advantage of an enemy's shift of troops from an unthreatened sector to the one under attack, but at Peachtree Creek this did not happen; each of Thomas's divisions dealt with the Confederate attack on its own. On the other hand, echelon assaults can lead to lack of coordination among the assailants, and this did occur; more than one Southern officer complained about absence of support on his flank.

In the end, Hood's telegram to Richmond fairly accurately conveyed the partial success his troops had achieved that day, as well as their ultimate repulse: "at 3 o'clock to-day a portion of Hardee's and Stewart's corps drove the enemy into his breast-works, but did not gain possession of them."

Sherman was about as terse. "The enemy sallied from his intrenchments and fell suddenly and heavily on our line," Cump wired General Halleck in Washington; "for two hours the fighting was close and severe, resulting in the complete repulse of the enemy."

This monument at Peachtree Creek, adorned with both a Civil War kepi and a World War I doughboy helmet, reads: "On this historic ground, here Confederate soldiers defended Atlanta and disputed the southward advance of Federal troops along Peachtree Road, July 19th, 1864. This memorial is a tribute to American valor, which they of the blue and they of the gray had as a common heritage. From their forefathers of 1776 and to the pervading spirit thereof which in the days of 1898 and the Great World Conflict of 1917-1918 perfected the reunion of North and South." (dd)

LEGGETT'S HILL

July 22, 1864, Blair's 17th A.C., McPherson's Army of the Tenn., was aligned S. of Logan's 15th astride the Ga. R. R. Leggett's div. of the 17th held the line from Logan's left, to & including the hill. An extension S. E. on Flat Shoals Rd. to Glenwood was occupied by the other division of the 17th A.C., under Giles Smith. Smith's div., outflanked by Cleburne's troops, was driven to the S. slope of Leggett's Hill. This was followed by concerted attacks on front, flank & rear by Cleburne's & Maney's divs. (Hardee's A. C.), together with Stevenson's (Cheatham's A. C.), a battle regarded as the major engagement of the Atlanta Campaign.

044-57   GEORGIA   HISTORICAL   COMMISSION   1955

The Fight for Bald Hill

CHAPTER FOUR

For many Atlantans, streetside historical markers are as close to the story of the Atlanta Campaign as they will get. In the early 1950s, the Georgia Historical Commission hired Atlantan Wilbur G. Kurtz to write the text for hundreds of metal markers it placed along roadways throughout north Georgia. In Fulton County alone (central Atlanta), more than 150 of these markers were installed. Kurtz not only wrote the copy, but for many tablets specified precisely where he wanted the state to set them. This one, "Leggett's Hill," was intended for Moreland Avenue at Trenton Street. Nowadays the intersection doesn't exist; it was bulldozed away during the construction of the city's downtown interstates. Fortunately, the marker survived; it stands a hundred yards south of its original site. The high ground was dubbed Leggett's for Brig. Gen. Mortimer Leggett's 3rd Division, XVII Corps, which held the position during the battle of July 22. (ahc)

The battle of Peachtree Creek had not even begun north of the city when McPherson's column east of Atlanta started making more trouble for Hood.

As his forces closed in on the city on July 19, Sherman instructed that any of his artillery batteries that got close enough should open bombardment of Atlanta. By noon of the 20th, Logan's XV Corps had advanced to two-and-a-half miles east of downtown. That allowed Capt. Francis DeGress's Illinois battery of 20-pounder Parrott rifled cannon to fire three rounds randomly into the city. Despite a postwar legend that the first Northern shell killed a little girl, DeGress's shots inflicted no casualties. Nevertheless, the explosion of Yankee shells in the city drove more residents to flee. Eventually only 3,000, maybe 4,000, non-combatants remained in Atlanta.

More threatening to Hood was the speed of the enemy's advance. Wheeler had but 3,500 troopers to oppose McPherson's 25,000. The Confederates deployed astride a ridge crossed by the Georgia Railroad. Wheeler's right rested on a "bald" (deforested) hill a mile south of the

Patrick Ronayne Cleburne, born in Ireland in 1828, was one of two foreign-born officers to become a major general in the Confederate army (the other was the Frenchman Camille de Polignac). After emigrating to the U. S. in 1849, he moved to Helena, Arkansas. With the coming of war, Cleburne rose in rank from colonel of the 15th Arkansas to brigadier before Shiloh. Promoted to major general in December 1862, he distinguished himself at Murfreesboro and Missionary Ridge, where his rearguard stand saved the trains of Bragg's retreating army. His division was widely hailed as one of the best and toughest in the Army of Tennessee. (loc)

Frank Preston Blair (1821-1875), born into a prominent Washington family (think Blair House in the capital), was the brother of Montgomery Blair, Lincoln's postmaster general. In St. Louis before the war, Blair rose as an outspoken opponent of slavery. He raised Missouri troops for the Union, was commissioned brigadier general in August 1862, and major general several months later. During the Vicksburg campaign, he led a division under William T. Sherman, who became his good friend. He led the XVII Corps throughout the Atlanta campaign. (wc)

Walter Q. Gresham, Indiana attorney and politician, became colonel of the 53rd regiment of Hoosier infantry. After Vicksburg, he was promoted to brigadier and put in charge of a division in the XVII Corps. On the afternoon of July 20, 1864, advancing on Atlanta from Decatur, Frank Blair was pushing his troops hard, as was XV Corps leader Black Jack Logan. Coming under enemy fire, Gresham was struck in the left leg below the knee. "It's too bad, Gresham," General Blair told him; "I was racing John Logan to get into Atlanta and you go and get shot." The wound sent him home to Indiana for the rest of the war. (wc)

railway, which became the objective of Frank Blair's XVII Corps. Brigadier General Walter Gresham's division pressed up against the Rebel position; Gresham took a bullet in the leg. (Today's Gresham Road in the area is named for him.)

Wheeler called for help. General Mackall at Hood's headquarters urged him to "hold at all hazards" and announced that one of Cheatham's brigades was being sent to him. That was still not enough, so Wheeler dispatched another plea later in the afternoon of the 20th. Hood responded by ordering to his aid Cleburne's division, which had not participated in the battle at Peachtree Creek.

During the night of July 20-21, Cleburne's infantry marched through the city and out to Wheeler's position east of it, reinforcing the cavalrymen upon the bald hill and strengthening their flimsy earthworks. At dawn, Federals shelled the hill, and at 8 a.m., infantry of Brig. Gen. Mortimer Leggett's division charged and took it. Cleburne's counterattack failed to recapture the bald hill. Leggett brought up artillery as the fight fizzled out around 11 a.m.

Federal casualties in the three-hour engagement totaled 700 for Leggett, 300 for Cleburne, and 50-100 for Wheeler. The Confederates had lost a key position, but had stopped McPherson's advance at least for the day.

Sherman was nonetheless delighted with McPherson's progress on July 21. The night before, he had urged him to be aggressive. "Still more good results will flow from your pressing hard," Cump had advised his friend. Mac had delivered with those good results with Leggett's capture of the hill, which curiously among some Civil Warriors still carries his name. "From this hill," Sherman informed Thomas, "he has an easy range of the town"—meaning artillery range.

The Union commander, as we shall see, very much looked forward to his cannon bombarding the city of Atlanta.

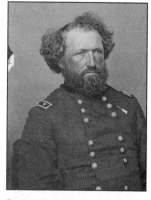

During the Vicksburg campaign, Brig. Gen. Mortimer D. Leggett shone as brigade commander in John Logan's division of McPherson's XVII Corps. He was given division command in November 1863. On the morning of July 21, 1864, Leggett was ordered to charge and take the bald hill atop which Rebels were blocking Federals' advance toward Atlanta. In a several hours' sharp fight, Leggett's troops took the position, then held it against Pat Cleburne's counterattack. As historian Gary Ecelbarger has written, "his successful assault and subsequent defense of Bald Hill was the reason that the height was renamed Leggett's Hill." (loc)

Ulysses S. Grant was a particular admirer of John Logan, the fighting politician without West Point training. "There is not a more patriotic soldier, braver man, or one more deserving of promotion in the Dept. than Gen. Logan," Grant wrote President Lincoln in February 1863, recommending Black Jack for major general. In the Vicksburg campaign, Logan's leadership at the battle of Champion Hill caused Grant to tell an aide, "Go down to Logan and tell him he is making history today." When the Rebel river fortress surrendered, Grant awarded Logan the post of honor, riding at the head of the Union troops marching into the city. (loc)

THE TROUP HURT HOUSE

The plantation house of Geo. M. T. Hurt, begun in the Summer of 1862, never completed & never occupied as a residence, stood on the site of the stone church. It faced the Decatur Rd. July 18, 1864. A sector of the outer line of Atlanta's defense works was located just E. of the house, which was used as hd'q'rs by the 10th S. Carolina regt. of Manigault's brigade. July 22. The same troops, having withdrawn to the city the night before, returned late afternoon & attacked the Federal forces occupying the position, capturing & holding it until driven out. This is the moment shown in the Cyclorama of the Battle of Atlanta.

GEORGIA HISTORICAL COMMISSION

Hood's Flank Attack of July 22

CHAPTER FIVE

Probably the most famous segment of the "Battle of Atlanta" Cyclorama is the two-story red brick house owned by George M. T. Hurt. Begun as a plantation house in mid-1862, well outside the Atlanta suburbs at the time, the dwelling was still unfinished when war came this way in July 1864. In the battle of July 22, Confederates broke through the XV Corps line here and unsuccessfully tried to fend off Yankee counterattacks before withdrawing. The house was damaged in the fighting, but stood at the end of it. A few days later, as Sherman shifted his forces from east to west of the city, Union lines changed. The Troup Hurt house, once north of the railway and behind Union trenches, now lay out in no-man's land. General Sherman himself issued orders to Gen. John M. Schofield on July 27: "If you don't occupy that brick house as an outpost, burn it." Schofield soon reported, "The brick house you refer to was burned this evening." Today the East Atlanta Baptist Church, as shown here behind the marker, stands on the site. (dd)

The gap between Thomas's and Schofield's armies on July 20, which Hood had termed "a serious blunder," had given the Confederate commander opportunity to attack Thomas's Army of the Cumberland on roughly equal terms. Now Sherman was about to commit an even more serious blunder that would give Hood and his army an even more promising prospect of victory.

Sherman was fixated on the destruction of the enemy's railroads. When he had led his Army of the Tennessee across Mississippi from Vicksburg to Meridian in February 1864, he bragged that his troops had destroyed 115 miles of track, 61 bridges and culverts, and 6,075 feet of wooden trestles. Now, outside of Atlanta, his infantry and cavalry had already torn up much of the track running east of the city through Decatur to Stone Mountain—a stretch of the Georgia Railroad the Rebels would never use again for the rest of the war.

That did not matter to Cump, who wanted even more of the railway to Augusta obliterated. Thus on July 21, Sherman ordered Brig. Gen. Kenner Garrard to take his cavalry

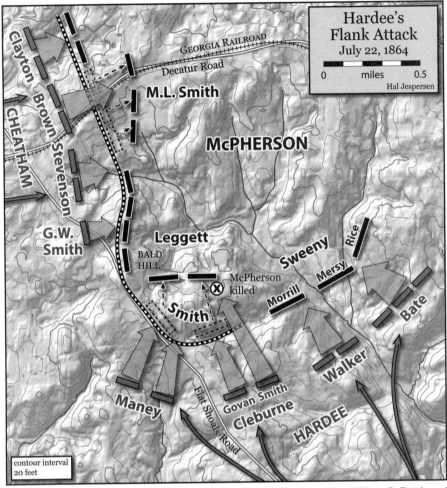

HARDEE'S FLANK ATTACK—Around noon on July 22, Hardee's lead divisions, William B. Bate's and William H. T. Walker's, discovered that far from rolling up the enemy flank, they were advancing straight against Yankee infantry deployed to meet them.

division riding off toward Covington, 35 miles east of Atlanta, burning railroad river bridges, destroying depots, and wrecking locomotives. Garrard got his troopers riding early in the afternoon of the 21st.

Problem was, Garrard's cavalry had been guarding the left (south) flank of McPherson's army as it pushed toward Atlanta. With his cavalry "eyes" gone, Mac started to worry the Rebels might try to raid behind his front and attack his supply trains at Decatur. He therefore ordered an infantry brigade there to guard the wagons. With great prescience late in the afternoon he sent warning to General Blair, whose corps held the army's left: "impress upon the command the importance of being on the alert at all times to repel an attack, especially about daybreak."

That's exactly what Hood hoped to do. On the afternoon of July 21, Wheeler brought news that the enemy left flank east of Atlanta was in the air. Hood quickly made plans to exploit the situation. All three of his infantry corps then occupied the outer defenses south of Peachtree Creek; they were to be brought into the Grant-Presstman perimeter during the night of July 21-22. Hardee's troops would keep marching—into the city, through it, and out by the main road to the southeast in an all-night march. Then they would turn to the northeast, marching beyond the enemy's flank and into their rear. Once there, Hardee's infantry were to wheel and attack the enemy. Wheeler's cavalry, accompanying the column, were to ride on to Decatur and attack the Yankee wagon train.

Hood's plan was definitely bold and ambitious—too much so. After marching all night, Hood expected that Hardee's troops could launch their assault in the morning of July 22. Nevertheless, in conference at Hood's headquarters the evening of the 21st, Hardee, Stewart, and Cheatham, together with Wheeler and G. W. Smith, all heard the commanding general explain his plan. Hood asked each officer if he understood his role; all assented.

The sight of Hardee's infantry marching through the city spooked a number of citizens, who assumed the army was abandoning Atlanta. Some soldiers, especially Wheeler's horsemen, noticed a number of residences were unoccupied. Their owners had fled, so pilferers

Born in Fredericksburg, Virginia, in 1817, Carter Littlepage Stevenson exemplifies the Confederate general who served throughout the war creditably but without stellar achievement. After West Point, Mexico, and old army service, Stevenson entered the Southern army commanding the 53rd Virginia. He was promoted brigadier in February 1862 and major general a half-year later. He was captured at Vicksburg, exchanged, and took charge of a division in the Army of Tennessee. Stevenson was finally paroled at Greensboro, May 1, 1865. An engineer after the war, he died in Fredericksburg and is buried in its city cemetery along with five other Confederate generals. (loc)

Brig. Gen. Manning F. Force (1824-1899) became one of Civil War medicine's hard-luck stories. Harvard graduate, Cincinnati attorney, Union colonel (20th Ohio, May 1862), he rose further after Vicksburg to command a brigade under Sherman. In the battle of July 22 for the bald hill, Force was shot through the mouth. The bullet entered below the left eye and exited under the right, carrying away part of the upper jaw. The patient not only survived but returned to duty three months later. After the war, Force resumed his successful law career, but in his last decade he experienced neurological effects of his wound: disturbed speech, facial twitching, gradual loss of his right leg, and loss of intestinal muscle control. After his death in 1899, his widow applied for a pension, which was denied because of inconclusive medical evidence. Force, however, was awarded the Medal of Honor in 1892 for his heroism in the battle. (loc)

plunged in. Streetside shops were plundered, too. Samuel P. Richards, a downtown bookseller, lamented the theft of his goods. "A lot of cavalry robbers broke into the stores and stole everything that they took a fancy to," he recorded in his diary. "They had sacks tied to their saddles," wrote a disgusted Confederate at the sight of some troopers on the 22nd, "and all through the day cavalrymen would be seen with their horses literally piled up and almost concealed by the plunder they had on them."

Hood's plan to attack McPherson's flank and rear offered as much prospect of a great Confederate victory as had Stonewall Jackson's flank attack on the XI Corps at Chancellorsville. There were important variances, however, that help explain the different outcomes of the two battles. Whereas Jackson's troops were able to sleep the night before and cook breakfast before beginning their march at 7 a.m. on May 2, Hardee's four divisions had to march all night, July 21-22. Cleburne's was not even able to leave its lines east of the city before midnight.

Jackson understood, thanks to a good map and help from local residents, the distance his men would have to march, 11 or 12 miles. Hood and Hardee markedly disagreed over their march-route. The commanding general grossly underestimated the distance Hardee would have to cover, even claiming in his memoir, "I considered Hardee's move one merely within the lines of our cavalry." Wheeler would show the way, and Hardee had only to follow; "no special quality, such as Jackson possessed, was required," Hood dismissively claimed.

Hardee was aware that Hood had handed him a tall order, and before leaving the city, he sought to change it. "My troops had been marching, fighting and working the night and day previous, and had little rest for thirty-six hours," he wrote later. He knew a morning attack on the enemy rear after a long night-march was impossible, so he stopped at Hood's headquarters and asked for discretion in launching the battle. Hardee later claimed he got it; Hood later disagreed.

More than the length of Hardee's march—which would eventually be measured as 13 to 15 miles— the essential element in explaining the outcome in his attack lay in the enemy's deployment. Jackson's target, the Federals of Howard's corps, did not expect the Rebel assault, and Stonewall spent a couple of hours positioning his infantry to strike the very flank of the enemy line. Hardee's was a completely different situation.

McPherson had already warned Frank Blair to be on the lookout for a Rebel attack. On the morning of July 22, sure enough, Union observers high in a tree spotted distant columns marching. McPherson ordered an infantry division—Tom Sweeny's, the same one that had flanked Johnston at Resaca—to the end of Blair's line, facing south against attack. Soon a brigade from Brig. Gen. John Fuller's division of the XVII Corps joined Sweeny. The Northerners were even able to start fortifying.

McPherson's precautions should have met with Sherman's approval, but they didn't. In fact, around 7:30 that morning, the commanding general sent Mac a note stating his wish that Dodge's troops not be placed to guard his flank but sent back to destroy more of the railroad to Decatur. McPherson rode to headquarters and talked Sherman out of it. Had he not, and had

Like his older brother George, Augustus Hurt was a gentleman farmer. He had his two-story plantation house built in 1858. Sometime before the Yankees came, Hurt and family left their property in the hands of a neighbor, Thomas Howard. When Sherman occupied it as his headquarters on July 22, he referred to it as the "Howard house." Theodore Davis, illustrator for *Harper's Weekly*, was with Sherman and, years later, drew this picture of the house for *Battles and Leaders*, possibly from a wartime sketch. Augustus Hurt's house survived the battle, but not the subsequent Federal occupation of the area. Decades after the war, Hurt wrote Atlantan Wilbur Kurtz, "the house was afterwards torn down by the soldiers and shacks were built of same." The house site is today on the grounds of the Carter Center and Jimmy Carter Presidential Library east of Atlanta. (hw)

On July 20, 1864, the four 20-pounder Parrotts of Capt. Francis DeGress's Battery H, 1st Illinois Light Artillery had pulled close enough east of Atlanta to lob several shells into the city—the first ones of Sherman's 37-day bombardment. On the 22nd, DeGress's battery supported Brig. Gen. Morgan L. Smith's division in this sector of Logan's XV Corps line, north of the railroad near the Troup Hurt house. Just before his guns were overrun by Arthur Manigault's Rebels, DeGress ordered his men to try to drag them to the rear. "But they were to heavy and my men were to much worn out," DeGress later wrote, so he had to leave his battery. It was recaptured in the Federal counterattack directed by Black Jack Logan. (dd)

the Rebels run over the Army of the Tennessee's left flank, W. T. Sherman would have stood to blame for a tactical myopia exceeding Joe Hooker's at Chancellorsville. Hooker was later relieved of army command; one may only imagine the future course of the war if Sherman had been relieved after a very-much possible Confederate triumph at Atlanta on July 22.

*   *   *

Hardee's troops, wearied by a night-march in July heat over dusty roads, were fagged even before the fight started. "I never saw as much straggling from our Corps," wrote a Tennessean in Maney's division, which at the end of Hardee's column had not gotten out of the city before three in the morning. One recent authority in the battle, Gary Ecelbarger, estimates that Hardee lost as much as 25 percent of his effective strength when exhausted men simply fell out of the line of march.

The Confederates' deployment for the attack did not go smoothly. At a point a few miles southwest of Decatur, Hardee concluded he had marched far enough so as to hit the enemy in flank. Besides, he reasoned, it was near noon, and the attack was way behind schedule. Hardee arrayed his divisions in line from west to east: Maney—Cleburne—Walker—Bate. Wheeler rode off to attack the Union wagon train.

As they wheeled off the Decatur Road, the Southern infantry trudged through woods and tangled briers. Walker and Bate found a miry swamp and big mill-pond ahead of them.

Trying to negotiate the lake in his front, Walker was shot from his horse, mortally wounded.

Then came the real surprise. "I was ignorant of what was in my front but believed the enemy was without defences," Bate remembered; "in this we were mistaken. . . . [T]he enemy had a strong force with breast-works and heavy batteries crowning the eminence." A Kentuckian in Bate's division expressed surprise that "we now discover that the yanks have two lines of battle in front of us, both strongly entrenched." The Federals were ready for battle, had brought up artillery, and when the Rebels charged, the Federals delivered a heavy, deadly fire. The Southerners were tired, diminished in number, and demoralized by the discovery that they had not surprised, much less outflanked, the enemy.

The uncoordinated attacks of Bate's and Walker's divisions, more or less piecemeal by brigade, fell apart in less than an hour, with the Confederates never having gotten close to Sweeny's and Fuller's lines.

Around noon, as Hardee's infantry started fighting, Wheeler's cavalry approached Decatur and it, too, was surprised. Guarding McPherson's trains were Union infantry and artillery, which repulsed the Southerners' first charge. Its second pushed the Yankees through town but not before the Federals were able to rush their wagons off to safety. Wheeler was about to pursue when Hardee called him back to the main fight.

*   *   *

General James McPherson watched as his men turned Bate and Walker back. Then he heard that there was a half-mile gap between Fuller's/Sweeny's position and the main XVII

"About 2 P.M. Genls Hood & M ride to rear Cheatham's line," recorded Lt. Thomas B. Mackall in his diary. The lieutenant was Hood's staff officer and nephew of Brig. Gen. William W. Mackall ("Genl M"), Hood's chief of staff. Thomas Mackall's journal is a great resource for students of the Atlanta campaign. It reposes at William & Mary—and remains unpublished—yet is often quoted in the literature. Hood rode out to east of the city and took a perch in the second-floor window of the house owned by James E. Williams. The site, in today's Oakland Cemetery (where this marker stands), was about two miles from the engagement and, as Mackall noted, just within the lines of Frank Cheatham's corps. Hood saw the battle smoke as Hardee's troops struggled to take the bald hill. Soon he ordered Cheatham's attack against the XV Corps, the last major Southern action in the battle of July 22. (dd)

Corps line. McPherson, with several staff members, rode westward to see for himself. At the same time, Cleburne's division was advancing against Blair's two divisions—Giles Smith's and Mortimer Leggett's, the latter of which held the bald hill. Daniel Govan's brigade charged so hard that the Southerners pushed back two brigades of Yankees and captured a six-gun battery before they were stopped.

Brigadier General James A. Smith's Texas brigade of Cleburne's division was surging through the Northern line-gap, and at about 1:15, they came upon McPherson's party riding through the woods. The Confederates called on the general to halt; he refused to, and turned his horse around. Captain Richard Beard, commanding the 5th Confederate Regiment, gave the order to shoot. History has it that Cpl. Robert Coleman of the 5th fired and brought the general down. Coleman's bullet struck McPherson in the back and passed through his chest. The general fell from his horse and was dead in a few minutes. His staff members escaped, and the Confederates rushed on.

Later, Federals returned to the scene and recovered McPherson's body, minus a few personal effects the Rebels had taken. The corpse was taken to Sherman's headquarters two miles to the north. "McPherson dead! Can it be?" Sherman exclaimed, deeply moved. James Birdseye McPherson thus became the 10th Union major general to die in battle—the last thus to fall during the war. As for Sherman's question, had he pondered it further, he may have realized that his friend Mac had died as result of his own decision to send Garrard's cavalry off railroad-raiding, which in turn had led Hood to conceive Hardee's flank assault.

*   *   *

After dispatching McPherson, Smith's Texans pushed on, overrunning an Illinois regiment before encountering the enemy in strength. Unsupported, Smith ordered his brigade to fall back. He took a wound just before a Northern countercharge speeded the Texans' retreat; the Federals took prisoners and colors of two regiments.

It was about 2 o'clock or a little after when Maney's division joined in support of Cleburne's attack against Giles Smith's division south of the bald hill. Brigadier General Otho F. Strahl's brigade shoved back a regiment of Iowans, then encountered a destructive fire from Col. Benjamin Potts's brigade, stalling its assault. Strahl was borne from the field, severely wounded.

Another of Maney's brigades forced back Col. William Hall's Iowans. As the Confederates pushed north astride the enemy's entrenched line, they were able to fire on the Yankees from both sides. Hall's troops had to jump over their parapets, then jump back to return the Rebels' musketry. The Confederate attack began to sputter out even as the Federals fell back upon the bald hill, which then became the focal point of the battle.

To break the stalemate, Cleburne assembled troops for a renewed assault, which began around 2:15. The Confederates charged hard, in places pressing up to the enemy works. At one point, Col. Harris Lampley of the 45th Alabama was actually grabbed by the collar and dragged across the earthen parapet as a prisoner. Yet the Southerners could not sustain their assault and began to fall back.

The bald hill itself, held by two Union brigades, was assailed by Brig. Gen. Mark Lowrey's brigade of Cleburne's division. One of the Federal brigadiers, Manning Force,

After Confederates abandoned their outer fortified line in the night of July 21-22, Federal forces pushed closer to Atlanta. The advance of the XV Corps allowed a Northern signal officer, Lt. Samuel Edge, to set up an observation platform in a tall pine tree behind the newly established Union line near the Troup Hurt house. On the morning of the 22nd, Edge saw distant dust clouds and deduced that they came from marching enemy infantry. At 10 a.m., he reported this to Generals Logan and McPherson. An hour later, he sent another report of "additional movements of an alarming nature." McPherson, already fearful of being attacked, thus had advance warning of the coming Rebel assault. (dd)

clutched a U. S. flag, rallying his men, when he was struck in the face by a rifle ball. He never lost consciousness as he was carried from the field. Years after the war, Force suffered degenerative neurological damage from his wound, but after his death, the U. S. government denied the widow a pension for having failed to provide enough medical evidence linking the general's war injury with his eventual demise.

*   *   *

Two decades after the war, U. S. army officers stationed in Atlanta resolved to raise a monument at the site of McPherson's death and bought this small tract of land. The War Department donated the cannon, which was set in a block of granite from nearby Stone Mountain. Appropriately, the small park is today located at the intersection of McPherson and Monument Avenues. (cm)

Both Sherman and Hood kept their distance from the battle of July 22. Sherman stayed at the Augustus Hurt house, in which McPherson's body lay, stretched out in the parlor on a yanked-down door. Hood left his downtown headquarters around 2 o'clock and rode to a hill near the Grant-Presstman line, where from the second story of a house, he could watch the battle. After having received a report from Hardee that his attack was stalled, Hood ordered Frank Cheatham's corps into the fight. Cheatham was occupying the works east of the city; with the enemy so heavily engaged around the bald hill, a Confederate assault against the enemy line northward offered successful prospects. Additionally, Cheatham's assault would deter the enemy from diverting XV Corps troops to reinforce the struggling XVII corps to the south.

Shortly after noon McPherson watched his troops repulse Rebel attacks. Then, hearing firing to the southwest, he headed in that direction. Unfortunately, he and his staff rode straight into the enemy advance. Confederates called for the Yankees to surrender. Instead, McPherson tipped his hat and turned his horse to escape. He was shot through the back and probably died just minutes after hitting the ground. Staff officers escaped and later returned to claim his body. Today, an upraised cannon and historic marker stand at the site. (loc)

Cheatham's three divisions marched eastward from their fortifications in an echelon attack from the right to left. The order this time was, first, Maj. Gen. Carter L. Stevenson's division, then Brig. Gen. John C. Brown's, finally Maj. Gen. Henry D. Clayton's on the left (north).

The assault began at 3:30 with lackluster results from Stevenson's troops. But Brig. Gen. Arthur M. Manigault's brigade of Brown's division, attacking near the Georgia Railroad, actually punched through the Yankee line, sending Brig. Gen. Joseph Lightburn's brigade packing for the rear and capturing the six guns of Battery A, 1st Illinois Artillery—the very same Parrott guns which, two days before, had lobbed the first shells into Atlanta. The Yankees fled the scene, causing Lt. Robert M. Gill of the 41st Mississippi to recall in a letter to his wife, "I never enjoyed a thing better in my life. We had the pleasure of shooting at Yankees as they ran without being shot at much."

"I never saw the like of Knapsacks, Blankets,

oil cloths and Canteens in my life," Gill observed; "our men supplied themselves."

By 4:30 p.m., Brown's troops occupied up to three-quarters of a mile of Yankee trenches, centered around the red brick house owned by Troup Hurt, a central feature in today's famous Cyclorama painting of the battle. To Brown's north, the attack of Clayton's division failed to achieve similar success. Then Gen. "Black Jack" Logan rallied his troops, called in reinforcements, and organized a counterattack. The Federals pressed hard, and Brown and Clayton ordered their divisions to withdraw to their original positions.

Theodore Davis drew this sketch on July 7, 1864, from a Federal observation platform when Sherman's forces were still north of the Chattahoochee. When published in *Harper's Weekly*, the caption identified Lt. Samuel Edge, XV Corps signal officer, as seated on the left. The observation post, which Edge set up near the Troup Hurt house early on July 22, would have offered a similarly panoramic view of the surrounding area. (hw)

But the battle was not yet over. Pat Cleburne put together enough troops to launch one final effort against the bald hill. The assault began at 6 p.m. The Southerners charged boldly, but Leggett's defenders were just as resolute—plus they had artillery and were well dug in. The Confederates surged to the very enemy works, where hand-to-hand fighting ensued. But the Yanks refused to budge, and the Rebs had to retire. At 8 o'clock, with the sun setting, the engagement finally ended.

* * *

In the eight-hour battle east of Atlanta— which has traditionally carried the city's name but in some narratives is called the battle of Bald Hill—the Confederates had achieved some temporary successes, driving back the Federals or at places puncturing their lines, taking prisoners and a dozen pieces of artillery.

Major General McPherson was dead, but so was Major General Walker.

Most significant, however, Hood's hoped-for rolling-up of the enemy flank, as Jackson had done a year earlier, failed, largely for two reasons. First, Hood ordered Hardee and his corps to do more than even ardent veterans could hope to achieve: a dawn attack after an all-night, long, hot march on the enemy *rear* (not merely flank). And second, McPherson expected to be attacked and took precautions against it, even against the wishes of his superior.

Sherman had done nothing to help the Federals' defensive tactical victory on July 22. In fact, he had brought on Hood's attacking battle by sending off the cavalry guarding his flank. Then, on the morning of the fight, Sherman had tried to undo the defensive measures McPherson

A native of Augusta, Georgia, William Henry Talbot Walker graduated from West Point in 1832. During the Mexican War, he was severely wounded at Molina del Rey. Posts in the U. S. army afterward included commandant of cadets at West Point in the mid-1850s. He was commissioned Confederate brigadier in May 1861. Five months later, serving in Joseph E. Johnston's army in Virginia, Walker resigned over a question of rank and seniority. In early 1863, he was called back into service as brigadier and promoted major general that June. Walker was known for his temper, which he showed on the morning of July 22 as he led his division into position for Hardee's attack. Finding a large mill pond blocking his route, he threatened to shoot his civilian guide before staff officers calmed him down. About noon, as his column neared the enemy, a Federal picket shot Walker, probably killing him instantly. (wc)(dd)

had taken to repulse Hood's attack. Once again, Cump had proven his mediocrity as battle leader. Without McPherson and some downright good luck, Sherman might have suffered a defeat as ignominious as Hooker's at Chancellorsville.

General Logan, who took over command of the Army of the Tennessee in the immediate wake of McPherson's death, counted his casualties on July 22 as 430 killed, 1,559 wounded and 1,733 missing, for a total of 3,722. Hardee's corps took the majority of Confederate casualties; his chief of staff put the toll at 3,299. Cheatham's corps lost up to another 2,000. With Wheeler's rather light loss, Hood's army incurred some 5,500 officers and men killed, wounded, and missing in the battle.

Contrasted to many other attacking battles, Hood's assault on July 22 resulted in a more balanced attacker/defender ratio (about 1.5 to 1) than seen elsewhere (*e.g*, Kennesaw Mountain, 4 or 5 to 1).

Neither army commander had complete casualty figures when he made his initial report of the battle. Hood chose to highlight his troops' success: "General Hardee, with his corps, made a night march and attacked the enemy's extreme left at 1 o'clock to-day; drove him from his works. . . . Major-General Cheatham attacked . . . at 4 p.m. [and] drove the enemy." Hood also overstated the number of enemy cannon and prisoners taken, giving the impression of victory. In Richmond, the news from Atlanta "diffused general joy through the community," newspapers reported. Even General Lee took notice of the initial reports of Hood's "glorious victory at Atlanta."

Sherman, of course, put a different cast on the engagement. Leggett and Smith had done "terrible . . . execution of the enemy's ranks"; after his line was broken, Logan counterattacked "in superb style." At the end of the day, the Rebels had retreated into their works, leaving their dead and wounded on the field. Sherman estimated their casualties would reach 8,000 men.

He was pleased with the day's results, but mourned McPherson's death. "He was a noble youth, of striking personal appearance, of the highest professional capacity," Sherman wrote of his friend, "with a heart abounding in kindness that drew to him the affections of all men."

Sherman's Bombardment and "General" Issues

CHAPTER SIX

W. T. Sherman shared a trait with many generals in the American Civil and other wars: he jumped to conclusions about events in the belief that the enemy was doing what he hoped they would do. This instance involved the withdrawal of Hood's three corps from their outer line of works south of Peachtree Creek during the night of July 21-22. Early next morning, Union pickets found the Rebel trenches empty and sent word back. Sherman leaped to the belief that Hood was giving up Atlanta.

He ordered Thomas's army to launch pursuit—but it was not a long one. With daylight, the Northerners found the enemy definitely ahead of them, positioned in their defensive works outside the city. Sherman revised his orders to Thomas: "press down close from the north and use artillery freely, converging on the town."

Thomas pressed his line south, and Union artillerymen placed their batteries about two miles from the center of the city. This meant their rifled cannon—10- and 20-pounder Parrotts and 3-inch rifles—could throw shells into downtown Atlanta. Schofield's army, northeast of the city, also

The Carter Center and Jimmy Carter Presidential Library are located on 33 acres of greenery inside of Atlanta's busy perimeter highway. "An oasis within the fast-paced metropolis of Atlanta," it has been called. In the 1920s, Wilbur Kurtz figured out that the wartime Augustus Hurt house had been located at then-176 Cleburne Avenue and marked it on maps. From them, we know that the Hurt house, Sherman's headquarters for several days in July, stood on the northeast grounds of the Carter campus. (ahc)

In the late 1920s, Atlanta's indefatigable historian Wilbur Kurtz found the earthen remnants of three unusually prominent artillery embrasures near then-Cherry and 11th Streets. He deduced they were sites of the three 4.5-inch rifled siege cannon that Sherman had placed in the XX Corps lines north of Atlanta, positioned to throw their thirty-pound shells into the heart of the city. This is the site today, on the northern fringes of the Georgia Institute of Technology campus. (ahc)

advanced, and his artillery got into range, as well. "July 22, moved in front of Atlanta," Capt. Joseph C. Shields of the 19th Ohio Battery reported; his 10-pounder Parrotts fired 187 shells into the city that day. Some cannon of the Army of the Tennessee also swung into action. "We threw quite a number of shots into the city," recorded an officer in a battery attached to Leggett's division.

Sherman's bombardment of Atlanta, begun on July 20, thus intensified 48 hours later. The commanding general himself issued the orders. "Good batteries will be constructed for the artillery," he instructed, "and a steady fire be kept upon the city of Atlanta."

Sherman probably knew there were still civilians in Atlanta, even though the stepped-up shelling caused more citizens to panic and board southbound trains for Macon. Yet several thousand non-combatants would remain in the city during Sherman's shelling, which would last 37 days. At times, the Northern commander willed himself to believe the civilians had evacuated. "The inhabitants, of course, have got out," he once told General Thomas. More likely, however, Sherman just did not care if they had or not. By this time, in the third year of the war, bombardment of an enemy-occupied city had become accepted practice. Grant was doing it at

Local historians long ago fixed the Federal IV Corps entrenched line as running along 10th Street, astride Peachtree. Old time residents even pointed to breastworks near Juniper and 11th Streets. Then came the Eisenhower interstate highways of the 1950s and the "downtown connector"—I-75 and I-85—confluing through the heart of the modern city. Civil War tourists today whiz by, passing the site of the Union positions in an eyeblink. (ahc) (ahc)

Petersburg; Union Brig. Gen. Quincy Gillmore was doing it at Charleston. Notably, Hood never issued any protest of Sherman's practice during the bombardment, in which he himself at his headquarters sometimes came under enemy shellfire.

While Federal artillery maintained the cannonade, Sherman pursued his plan for capturing the city. His troops had cut the railroad to Augusta, and Union cavalry raiding in Alabama had wrecked the rail link to Montgomery. That left only the line from Atlanta to Macon for Hood to bring in supplies for his troops and the people in the city. The Macon & Western thus became Sherman's next objective. Even though McPherson/Logan's army was closer to it than was the right flank of Thomas's army near the Chattahoochee, Sherman planned to swing the Army of the Tennessee around behind Schofield

Funny thing about urban history: it tends to move around. In the mid-1950s, the state historical commission set this marker for the Augustus Hurt plantation at the intersection of Copenhill and Carmel Avenues. A generation later, however, the street intersection was obliterated in development of the big Jimmy Carter complex. This marker, which refers to the Confederate fortifications "on E. slope of this hill," is off; the marker has been moved—but at least it's still standing today, near the Carter Presidential Library. (ahc)

and Thomas, marching west of the city and southward to cut the railroad somewhere between Atlanta and East Point (so named as the eastern terminus of the line running to Montgomery).

Before he began his next phase of operations, Sherman had to find a replacement for the slain McPherson. Jack Logan as senior corps commander had been entitled to take initial charge of the Army of the Tennessee, but he was a "political" general, and Sherman believed that high positions should go to West Pointers. Major General Joseph Hooker, commander of the XX Corps, considered himself entitled to the post; after all, he had led the Army of the Potomac the year before—until Lincoln relieved him as Lee marched into Pennsylvania. But "Fighting Joe" was vain and could be uncooperative, and Sherman did not much care for him. When George Thomas voiced objection to Logan's appointment and threw his support to Maj. Gen. Howard, Sherman accepted the recommendation. Howard's appointment to lead the Army of the Tennessee was announced on July 26. Major General David Stanley would take over the IV Corps.

"Black Jack" was disappointed, but decided to stay on with the army. Hooker did not. Expressing resentment at being overridden by an officer junior in seniority—Howard had led the XI Corps when Hooker had commanded the army—Hooker submitted his resignation. Sherman snatched it up right away.

Hood had a few "general" issues of his own. Rather than replace the late Major General Walker, Hood decided to break up his division and apportion the brigades among the rest of Hardee's corps. Frank Cheatham had taken temporary command of Hood's corps, but Hood requested Lt. Gen. Stephen D. Lee to be brought from Mississippi. The latter arrived in

The Battles for Atlanta

Between July and Sept. 1864, during the American Civil War, U.S. and Confederate armies struggled for control of Atlanta, the major manufacturing center and railroad hub of the Deep South. Four inconclusive battles occurred inside the present day I-285 Perimeter: Peachtree Creek (July 20), Atlanta (July 22, fought in part in the area of this marker), Ezra Church (July 28); and Utoy Creek (August 6). Unwilling to attack the city's strong defenses, U.S. forces swept west and then south and at Jonesboro (August 31 - Sept. 1) cut the last railroad supplying Atlanta, forcing the Confederates to abandon the city. The fall of Atlanta on Sept. 2, 1864, assured the re-election of Abraham Lincoln and the final defeat of the Confederacy.

Erected for the Civil War 150 Commemoration by the Georgia Historical Society, the Georgia Battlefields Association and the Georgia Department of Economic Development

51-8

The war's sesquicentennial prompted the Georgia Historical Society, headquartered in Savannah, to place markers across the state. This one, standing on the grounds of the Carter Center, summarizes the fighting around the city in July 1864 and Sherman's success in cutting the Macon railroad on August 31. Unfortunately, this text errs in stating that the battle of Jonesboro, August 31-September 1, forced Hood to abandon Atlanta. Troops of the Federal XXIII Corps reached and broke the railroad eight miles north of Jonesboro mid-afternoon of the 31st, before the Confederate attack at Jonesboro had been repulsed. When Hood learned that his last supply lifeline was cut, he ordered preparations for the abandonment of Atlanta. (ahc)

Atlanta on July 26, and Cheatham returned to his division.

Hood also received another Confederate general officer in those days. On July 24, Gen. Braxton Bragg arrived in Atlanta and proceeded to Hood's headquarters, the home of John S. Thrasher on Whitehall Street. Brigadier General Mackall, who had stayed on as Hood's chief of staff after Joe Johnston's removal, resented Bragg's role in the affair. When Bragg walked onto the Thrasher house porch and extended his hand, Mackall refused to take it. Within 30 minutes,

What was once the area of "Fort Hood" and the Ephraim Ponder house is now along Tech Parkway and Marietta Street. The street sign "Bump Ahead" is ironic; back in 1864, Federals staring at the Rebels' huge earthen fortress at the northwest salient of their earthworks would definitely have seen a "bump ahead." (ahc)

This photo shows Confederate fortifications northwest of the city. George Barnard photographed this scene after Atlanta fell in early September; his camera was pointed eastward from the sandbagged Fort Hood. The two-story white stucco house of Ephraim and Ellen Ponder stands in the distance; it was unoccupied when fighting came this way. Outbuildings have been stripped of their wood for palisades. The chevaux-de-frise and abatis were never tested by a Federal infantry assault. (loc)

he was relieved of his post. Hood appointed Brig. Gen. Francis A. Shoup, his chief of artillery, to succeed Mackall. He then moved Col. Robert Beckham to command the army's artillery.

A thornier problem involved William J. Hardee. He had taken criticism from Hood for Peachtree Creek, and after the battle of July 22, Hood began to charge him with not having followed his orders to march completely into the enemy's rear. (As we have seen, Hardee launched his assault when he thought he had gained the enemy army's *flank*.) More tellingly, it became apparent that Hardee had borne some resentment at seeing Hood promoted over him to command the army. To be sure, Hardee had declined to succeed Braxton Bragg the previous December, and thus had been passed over by President Davis and his Cabinet in July. But Hardee seemed to hanker for the command after all. "The President is endeavoring to create the impression that in declining the command at Dalton, I declined it for all time," Hardee wrote Mackall after the

Located just behind Confederate entrenchments three-quarters of a mile northwest of Atlanta's city limits, the Ponder house became a haven for Southern sharpshooters. It was the target of Federal artillery on August 9, when a Northern officer observed "the house had a large hole knocked in it besides being riddled." George Barnard took this photograph during the Federal occupation of Atlanta. Wilbur Kurtz believes that the Ponder house was destroyed by Federal troops marching into Atlanta ca. November 13-14, preparatory to setting out on Sherman's march to the sea. (loc)

George Barnard took more than a dozen pictures of the "first Fort east of the W&A R.R." We know the position as Confederate fort X or Fort Hood, at the northwest corner of Atlanta's fortifications. The Union gun crew stands at their post for the cameraman. The top of Barnard's portable darkroom, a light-proof tent in which he developed his glass plates, is slightly visible beyond the parapet. (loc)

latter had left the army. John B. Hood had come to Johnston's army as junior corps commander, but Hardee seemed to resent Johnston's reliance upon him. On June 20, Hardee confided to his wife Mary that he had just left army headquarters, where he saw Johnston and Hood in the act of laying plans. "From what I can see," Hardee seemed to mope, Hood "is doing most of it."

For all of these reasons, Hardee had become unhappy serving under Hood and wanted out. He asked Bragg to transfer him from Hood's command. Both Hood and Bragg favored the move, and so recommended to Jefferson Davis.

The president, however, took no action on Hardee's request.

Ezra Church

CHAPTER SEVEN

On July 25, Sherman issued orders for his swing around Atlanta. Before dawn of the 27th, Howard's army would withdraw from its position east of the city, march behind Schofield and Thomas, and fall in, corps by corps, beyond the Army of the Cumberland's right flank, extending it to the south. The Army of the Ohio would become the army group's left.

Sherman's troop movement began early on the 27th with the wagon wheels and artillery sack-wrapped to muffle noise. But within hours of the march's start, Confederate cavalry alertly reported it to headquarters. Hood informed Wheeler, "indications are that the enemy will attack our left."

Yet the Confederate commander had no intention of receiving the enemy's attack; he planned to launch one of his own. With Howard's army pushing southward west of the city, Hood saw opportunity to strike the enemy in flank. On the afternoon of July 27, he instructed Lee to prepare his corps for action, and that evening, he called both Lee and Stewart to his headquarters and explained his plan. While Hardee's corps and Smith's

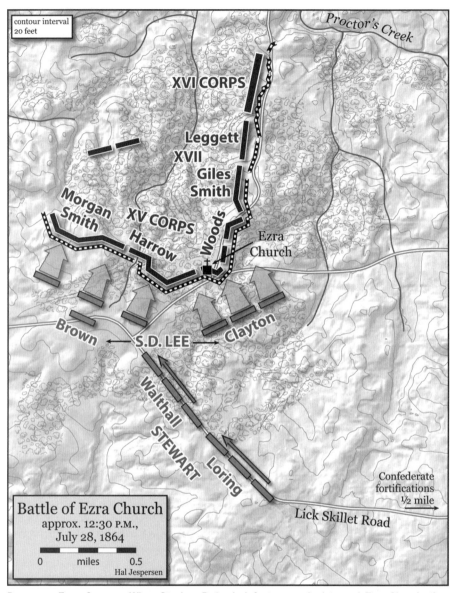

BATTLE OF EZRA CHURCH—When Stephen D. Lee's infantry marched toward Ezra Church, they found the Yankees were already there, expecting them. Lee decided he had no choice but to attack.

militia held the city's entrenchments, Lee was to march out from the city the next morning and seize an important crossroads named Lick Skillet, toward which the enemy column was known to be heading. Lee would dig in, await the Federals' approach, and hold them at bay. Stewart was ordered then to lead his infantry out, pass behind and beyond Lee's troops, then on July 29, march around the enemy's right flank and attack. Hood was showing the same predilection for flank attack he had the week before, east of Atlanta. This time, west of the city, he hoped for better results.

They were not to come. Howard, newly assigned to command the Army of the Tennessee, proved to be as cautious and foresightful as his predecessor. Even though Sherman did not think the Rebels would attack, Howard carefully extended his line division by division, so by late morning of July 28, the three corps were deployed on a north-south ridge whose southmost flank neared the Lick Skillet road. There, near a Methodist chapel called Ezra Church, Howard refused his line to the west with his three divisions, Charles Woods's, William Harrow's and Morgan Smith's. The Federals held high ground on a ridge and piled logs and rails—and on Woods's front, even church pews—into some manner of fortification. They were thus poised to face a Rebel assault, just as Tom Sweeny's division had been in the battle of July 22.

Before noon, contact with Rebel cavalry confirmed Howard's apprehensions that he

Without military training, Alabama lawyer Henry D. Clayton became colonel of the 39th Alabama and fought well enough at Murfreesboro to win promotion to brigadier in the spring of 1863. Leading his brigade in the Atlanta Campaign, he was raised to major general and given Peter Stewart's division when the latter became corps commander on July 7. (loc)

Theodore R. Davis, field artist for *Harper's Weekly*, accompanied Sherman's armies in the Atlanta Campaign. "General Sherman's campaign. Battle of Ezra's Church (General Wood's division), July 28, 1864," appeared in the Harper's issue of August 27. This woodcut engraving, rendered from the sketch Davis mailed to New York from Atlanta, shows Brig. Gen. Charles Woods's division of the XV Corps firing on Brig. Gen Alpheus Baker's Alabama brigade near Ezra Church—the area of today's Mozley Park. (loc)

would be attacked. Smith's and Harrow's divisions were ordered to dig in.

This was clearly not the situation Steve Lee anticipated when his infantry approached the area. Red Jackson reported that the Yankees were ahead, but he thought they were not in force. Lee assumed they also would have just neared Lick Skillet and had barely entrenched. Thus, even though Hood's orders called only for a defensive deployment awaiting Stewart's flank attack, Lee quickly decided to launch his own assault—a frontal one—on the enemy. "I believed that he would yield before a vigorous attack," he later explained. Lee did not even send couriers to army headquarters about his intentions.

To be sure, Stephen D. Lee was new to corps command in the Army of Tennessee, but his errors cannot be fully ascribed to his inexperience. He sent in his soldiers as they came up, leading to uncoordinated and piecemeal attacks. Worse, as Stewart's troops began to arrive, he threw them in, too. Stewart, who knew Hood's plan, might have objected, but he, too, was relatively new to corps command.

The battle of Ezra Church, fought three miles west of Atlanta, resulted in the one thing the Confederate commander had not intended: a frontal infantry assault upon an entrenched enemy. Three of John C. Brown's brigades attacked Morgan Smith's division. Only on the Confederates' far left did they gain some success with capture of a hill, which a Federal counterattack retook. Lee sent in one of Henry Clayton's brigades,

One of the state Civil War Centennial Commission's metal plaques mounted at Mozley Park shows Logan's XV Corps forces arrayed in a V crossing Mozley (now MLK) Drive. Brown's, Walthall's, Clayton's, and Loring's divisions are shown attacking the western face of the V. Modern cartographers of the battle offer different details; remember, this metal map reflected scholarship of fifty years ago. (ahc)

which advanced a little then hit the ground to exchange musketry with Harrow's and Woods's troops. After that, Clayton sent in another brigade, which was quickly repulsed.

Lee then ordered Arthur Manigault's brigade (Brown's division) to advance against Morgan Smith's line. Twice, Manigault's troops surged up the slope; twice, they fell back. When Stewart arrived with his lead division, Edward Walthall's, this too went in around 2 p.m. against Smith. His men charged vigorously, but the Federals fought back with equal stubbornness. Without support on his right—Loring's division was just coming up—Walthall ordered his troops to retire. The battle thus sputtered out when both Stewart and Loring were wounded.

The lopsided Union victory at Ezra Church was reflected in the two sides' uneven casualties: 632 Federals killed, wounded, and missing; and some 600 Confederates killed and another 2,200 wounded or missing.

* * *

That night, both Sherman and Hood received news of the day's fighting. Sherman explained Howard's defensive victory accurately: "our men were partially covered, while the enemy were exposed." Hood's report to Richmond was less truthful, in large measure because Lee dispatched inaccurate reports from the battlefield. Hood had sent Lee a reminder as early as noon that he was not to launch an attack unless "the enemy should make an assault upon our left." Shortly thereafter, Shoup informed Hardee that Lee was directed "not to attack unless the enemy exposes himself in attacking us." Lee seems to have sent some word back to headquarters that he indeed was under attack.

Brig. Gen. John C. Brown, commanding a division in S. D. Lee's corps, reported matter-of-factly on his troops' unsuccessful attack: "I formed . . . and instantly moved forward. The enemy's skirmishers were encountered at the road and his advance line a little beyond . . . It was routed and driven 500 or 600 yards and took refuge behind intrenchments. The woods were so dense that these works were not discovered until my line was upon them. In many places the works were carried, but the enemy re-enforced so rapidly and with such an immensely superior force, that my troops were driven with great slaughter from them." Brown reported 807 killed, wounded, and missing for his four brigades—about a fifth of the troops engaged. (lwc)

Brig. Gen. Morgan L. Smith's 2nd division, XV Corps held the right of Howard's line at Ezra Church against the attack of John C. Brown's division. It was "the most persistent and bloody attempt to dislodge us from our position and turn our right that I have ever witnessed," Smith wrote after the battle. (wc)

That night, Shoup recorded in his journal, "about 1 p.m. the enemy, who had massed a heavy force near Ezra Church on our left, advanced for the purpose of driving us from Lick Skillet road." Only in this light can Hood's subsequent messages to Lee be understood: "hold the enemy in check" (2:20 p.m.); "hold the enemy" (3:25 p.m.); "not to allow the enemy to gain upon you anymore" (4 p.m.).

In the battle of Ezra Church, Howard's infantry were clearly not advancing against Lee, but Hood did not try to set things straight in his telegram that night to Richmond. "The enemy commenced extending his right about 8 this morning, driving in our cavalry," Hood wrote. "Lieutenant Generals Stewart and Lee were directed to hold the Lick Skillet road for the day with a portion of their commands. About 1:30 o'clock a sharp engagement ensued with no decided advantage to either side. We still occupy Lick Skillet road." Hood was shamefully wrong in his last two statements. No disadvantage is more decided than a bloody battlefield repulse. And S. D. Lee certainly did not still hold the Lick Skillet road;

THE UNION DISPOSITIONS

150 years ago, Atlantans were talking about a national military park preserving the three battlefields of July 1864. In the 1930s, U. S. War Department engineers drew a map of how Peachtree Creek, Atlanta, and Ezra Church could all be commemorated with the purchase of just 48 acres and the erection of a marker at each of the three proposed parks. The money, estimated at $315,000 at the time, was never found. Thus, instead of a federal military reservation at Ezra Church, we have today Hiram Mozley city park. And instead of a stirring monument to American bravery in the battle fought west of the city, we have five wordy plaques from the 1960s, such as this one. (ahc)

after the battle, his infantry retreated but still covered the railroad to East Point.

At least the Confederates' repulse at Ezra Church temporarily halted Howard's southward advance on the vital rail line. The men in the ranks, however, dwelt more on the battle's casualties. "We lost a great many men for mity little gain," an Alabaman wrote on the 29th. An Arkansas officer asserted, "this Battle Discouraged our men Badly."

A story passed around among both Southerners and Northerners that a Yankee called out to a Rebel across the field, "Well, Johnny how many of you are left?" Johnny Reb was said to have answered, "Oh, about enough for another killing."

Brig. Gen. William H. "Red" Jackson (1835-1903) brought his cavalry division to the Army of Tennessee in May 1864 as part of Leonidas Polk's reinforcement of Joe Johnston. On July 28, Jackson's troopers were contesting the Yankees' march toward Lick Skillet. When S. D. Lee came up with his infantry, Jackson told him he thought that the enemy force in front of them was small (it was not). At least partly on the basis of Jackson's report, Lee concluded that "the enemy's works were slight, and besides they had scarcely gotten into position." So, he ordered the assault that began the battle of Ezra Church. (wc)

Atlanta's two major Confederate monuments stand in cemeteries: Oakland (statue dedicated in 1874) and Westview (1889). Westview Cemetery was not a wartime burial ground, having been established in 1884. The Confederate soldiers buried here, encircling the monument, were postbellum residents of Atlanta and died here well after the war. Inscriptions on the base of the marble statue come from the Bible ("nation shall not lift up sword against nation") and an ex-Confederate's poem ("a storm-cradled nation that fell"). (dd)

The McCook-Stoneman Cavalry Raid

CHAPTER EIGHT

"It is time we heard something of our cavalry," Sherman wrote General Schofield on July 29, and indeed it was. Kenner Garrard's cavalry division, sent off on July 21, had returned three days later, having burned railroad bridges across two rivers near Covington and tearing up a half-dozen miles of track. Southerners never attempted to repair the damage; rail connection between Atlanta and Augusta would be out for the rest of the war. Still, Sherman wanted more.

Like many other Civil War generals, Sherman clung to the belief that cavalry raids on railroads could inflict significant, campaign-altering damage. They seldom did: not once in the Eastern Theater and out west only twice—John Hunt Morgan in Tennessee, July 1862; Earl Van Dorn and Nathan Bedford Forrest in Mississippi, December 1862. In the case of the Georgia Railroad, it was the rail-wrecking of McPherson's infantry, not Union cavalry, that took out the rail line east of Atlanta.

Nonetheless, Sherman decided to send two strong mounted columns against the Rebels' Macon & Western (M&W). He drew up plans

Joe Wheeler became a local hero when his cavalry defeated McCook's Yankee raiders threatening Newnan, Georgia, in late July 1864. This marker, south of town at Old Corinth and Millard Farmer Roads, reads, "GEN. JOS.WHEELER, C.S.A. ROUTED GEN. E. M. McCOOK U.S.A. JULY 30TH 1864, CAPTURING 500 OF HIS MEN NEWNAN CHAPTER U. D. C. 1908." (hp)

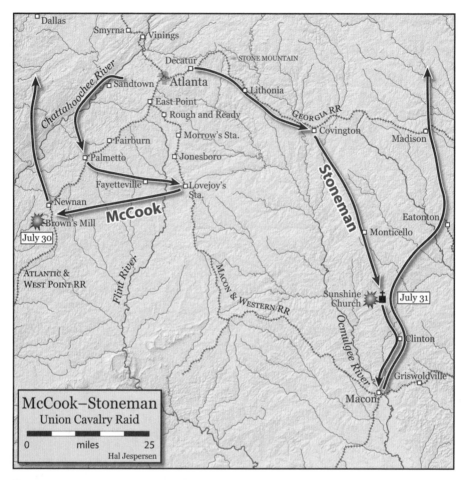

MCCOOK-STONEMAN UNION CAVALRY RAID—Cump Sherman learned the hard way what other Civil War commanders learned, too: that cavalry raids alone could not effectively cut enemy railroad lines. Edward McCook's and George Stoneman's twin columns failed to knock out Hood's Macon line for more than two days.

for Brig. Gen. Edward McCook and Maj. Gen. George Stoneman to lead their cavalry divisions in two separate directions to pounce on the M&W near Lovejoy's Station, two dozen miles south of Atlanta. Stoneman was to set out east of the city, through and beyond Decatur, then ride south to rendezvous at Lovejoy's with McCook, whose route would be down the Chattahoochee southwest of Atlanta, across it *via* Palmetto to the meeting point with Stoneman. There, Sherman hoped his troopers could tear up at least several miles of track and pull down telegraph wires.

The raiders were to ride out on the morning of July 27. Before departing, Stoneman asked Sherman if he could tack on another mission to the railroad raid. After Lovejoy's, could he ride farther south to Macon, attack the garrison there, and free the 1,500 Union officers known to be confined there? If that went well, could he ride another 55 miles southwest and attempt to free the much larger POW population at Andersonville? With this proposed glory-seeking, George Stoneman was trying to rebuild his reputation; a year earlier he had been relieved as cavalry commander in the Army of the Potomac.

Sherman gave his OK—but only after Stoneman hit the railroad at Lovejoy's.

Sherman was launching the biggest cavalry raid of the campaign to date. Five thousand troopers rode in two columns—2,144 with Stoneman, 3,000 with McCook. They started out on schedule, before dawn of July 27. The next day, McCook took time to wreck a couple of miles near

Brown's Mill Battlefield. Both of Edward McCook's and George Stoneman's cavalry raids were defeated by Confederates on July 30-31 in the battles of Sunshine Church, near Macon, and Brown's Mill, near Newnan. While there is no historical park at Sunshine Church battlefield, Brown's Mill is preserved by a Coweta County-owned park established about eight years ago. Six colorful panels describing the action were written by Dr. David Evans, author of *Sherman's Horsemen: Union Cavalry Operations in the Atlanta Campaign* (1996). (hp)

Brown's Mill Battlefield. "Sherman's primary strategy was to strike Hood's supply lines," the marker explains. By July 25 Union cavalry had cut Atlanta's railroads to Augusta and Montgomery, leaving only the Macon & Western. Sherman determined to send two mounted columns by separate routes to converge on Lovejoy's Station well south of Atlanta, wreck the railroad, then ride back to the army. They were to set out July 27—the day Sherman began marching the Army of the Tennessee around Atlanta toward Ezra Church. (hp)

Brown's Mill Battlefield. After destroying 2 ½ miles of track at Lovejoy's, McCook's column trudged westward through the night of July 29-30. Approaching Newnan, the Federals found Rebels ahead of them, with the town stoutly defended by Brig. Gen. Philip Roddey's 600 dismounted cavalrymen, who just happened to be en route from Alabama as reinforcements for Wheeler. McCook led his division south to avoid a fight, but soon ran into more Rebels as Wheeler, pursuing from the east, directed slashing attacks against the Union rear and flank. (hp)

Roddey's command, with walking wounded from Newnan hospitals, marched in to strengthen Wheeler's lines as the Confederates came close to enveloping McCook's force. With Rebels all around him, and his men nearly out of ammunition, McCook determined to try to break for the Chattahoochee. Some Yankees made it; others failed to cut their way out. Wheeler's men gathered in hundreds of prisoners on the field, and even more later that night as they pursued McCook's fleeing horsemen toward the river. (hp)

Palmetto of the Atlanta & West Point Railroad, even though Maj. Gen. Lovell Rousseau's raiders had recently cut the link to Montgomery. Later McCook's column came upon a Rebel wagon train; the Federals burned 500 wagons, captured the teamsters, and sabered 800 mules. On July 29, McCook struck the railroad at Lovejoy's and carried out Sherman's orders, tearing up two-and-a-half miles of track, cutting five miles' length of telegraph, and burning two supply trains headed for Hood's army. Having completed his mission, McCook and his cavalry did not wait on Stoneman, but headed west for a return to the army.

Stoneman, though, was *not* following orders. He did not even head toward Lovejoy's, but rode straight for Macon. He approached the city on the 30th. Garrisoning it, under command of Maj. Gen. Howell Cobb, were

a thousand Georgia militia, sundry regulars and home guards— maybe 2,000-2,500 men in all. Stoneman ordered a tentative advance on Rebels holding a blockhouse, but soon gave up trying to break into Macon. He ordered his column to start riding back north.

After Wheeler learned that two enemy mounted columns were heading to break the Macon Railroad, he split his forces. While he set out after McCook, he dispatched three brigades, 1,300 troopers, under Brig. Gen. Alfred Iverson to catch up with Stoneman. Wheeler closed in on McCook July 30. Full-blown battle erupted three miles south of Newnan, surging and rocking for several hours. At one point the 8th Iowa charged through the Southern lines, captured the horse holders and mounts of Brig. Gen. Lawrence S. "Sul" Ross's brigade, then snared Ross himself and scores of prisoners. Confederate counterattacks not only freed Ross but captured much of the 8th and its brigade commander, Col. Thomas Harrison. (hp)

Hours after the Yankees had ridden away from Sherman's flanks, Hood had authorized Wheeler to launch pursuit. Wheeler took two mounted brigades to ride after McCook and sent another three under Brig. Gen. Alfred Iverson to chase down Stoneman. On July 31, Iverson's force was 12 miles north of Macon, blocking Stoneman's route. The Federal commander ordered a charge, which failed to dislodge the Rebels. Hearing that Secesh from Macon were riding after him, Stoneman feared entrapment

In the spring of 1862, Macon authorities turned their fairgrounds into a fifteen- to twenty-acre prison stockade. After the establishment of Camp Sumter/Andersonville as a prison for Union enlisted men early in 1864, Camp Oglethorpe/Macon took in Federal officers. At the time of Stoneman's raid, about 1,300 were imprisoned here. (ahc)

On July 29, as Stoneman approached Macon, Confederate Maj. Gen. Howell Cobb, commander of the C. S. District of Georgia, scrambled to gather a defensive force. When Stoneman finally advanced against the city from the east on the morning of the 30th, Cobb stood in his way with a hastily assembled crowd of some 2,000 state militia, convalescent C. S. soldiers, local defense companies, and citizen volunteers. They were largely untried in battle, but they had artillery and held a hilltop position crowned by a blockhouse. The Federals advanced in several charges, but Cobb's line held. A disheartened Stoneman withdrew in mid-afternoon, giving up hope of riding down to free the beleaguered thousands at Camp Sumter, fifty miles to the southwest. Instead, he sent his troops retreating back toward Atlanta. (loc)

Brig. Gen. Edward M. McCook was one of the legendary "fighting McCooks'" of Ohio. One brother and two cousins had been serving with him as officers in Sherman's army. *Had been*, for Brig. Gen. Daniel, Jr., was now dead from wounds at Kennesaw Mountain. Edwin S., colonel of the 31st Illinois, was out sick, and Anson G., commanding the 2nd Ohio, had been ordered to Chattanooga for the mustering out of his regiment. Edward M. alone would now carry on the family's fighting tradition. (loc)

West Pointer George Stoneman had served out in Texas with the famed Second Cavalry (George Thomas, John B. Hood and William J. Hardee had been fellow officers). As cavalry chief for the Army of the Potomac, he had been replaced in May 1863 after undistinguished operations in the Chancellorsville campaign. Then he had been shoved out west after nearly a year's desk duty in Washington. With his career under a cloud, Stoneman sought glory and a refurbished reputation— hence his request to Sherman that he be given a chance to liberate Union prisoners kept at Macon and Andersonville. (loc)

and ordered two of his brigades to ride off as best they could. With the remainder of his force, he tried to break out, failed, and surrendered himself and some 700 of his men.

Iverson, who had disgraced himself as infantry brigadier in Lee's army on the first day of Gettysburg, managed to recoup something of his reputation in the battle of Sunshine Church, fought July 31 northeast of Macon. George Stoneman, who had sought to recoup his reputation by freeing Northern prisoners of war in central Georgia, failed, except in one unbecoming aspect. Surrendering to Iverson, Stoneman became the highest-ranking Union general to be captured by Confederate forces during the war. Those of his command who managed to escape, banged up again by Rebels near Athens on August 3, rode back into Union lines "stiff, sore and worn out."

Wheeler with his cavalrymen reached Lovejoy's late on July 29, witnessing the enemy's destruction just hours before. The next day, the Confederates caught up with McCook near Newnan at a place called Brown's Mill. As Stoneman had done, McCook panicked, feared encirclement, and ordered everyone to escape as they could. The Southerners captured hundreds of the enemy, leaving McCook and his survivors to limp back to Sherman's army.

Neither McCook nor Stoneman tried to hide the failure of their joint expedition. "My loss very heavy," the former reported. "We were whipped," announced Stoneman, writing from the very officers' prison in Macon that he had hoped to liberate. Together, the two commanders' losses on their raid totaled 2,559 officers and men: 50 percent of the number who had set out on July 27.

Hood and his staff were naturally delighted at Iverson's and Wheeler's success. "Good news has flowed in from all distant points," Shoup recorded on August 1. One of these was Lovejoy's Station, where the Confederates had repaired McCook's rail-damage in two days.

Sherman took the news of his cavalry's defeat very shakily. "I can hardly believe it," he admitted to General Halleck. Given McCook's and Stoneman's losses and the only slight damage done to the Rebels' railroad, Sherman was forced to acknowledge that sending off his cavalry had been "a military mistake."

After disgracing himself at Gettysburg, Brig. Gen. Alfred Iverson was transferred to Georgia. In the Atlanta campaign, he led a cavalry brigade under Wheeler. As Stoneman rode away from Macon, fifteen miles north on Sunday morning, July 31, he found Iverson's force waiting for him at a country chapel known as Sunshine Church. The Rebels were in a strong position, dug in with guns, but Stoneman attacked anyway. Repeated Union charges failed as Iverson sent men around both flanks. Fearing encirclement, the Federals panicked. Near 4 p.m., Stoneman ordered two of his brigades to cut their way out while he held ground with the third. After most of his force rode away, Stoneman surrendered. All told, Confederates rounded up 500 prisoners, a thousand horses, plus two Northern field pieces. They counted upward of 250 Union dead and wounded, against 50 Southern casualties. Iverson, as tarnished in reputation as his enemy Stoneman, had redeemed himself with a brilliant little victory at Sunshine Church. (loc)

Hood's Railroad Defense Line and the Fight at Utoy Creek

CHAPTER NINE

Sherman had learned the hard lesson that in the American Civil War, mounted troops raiding behind enemy lines could not achieve anything more than temporary breaks in the enemy's railroad system. The inevitable conclusion was that the infantry would have to do the job.

As McCook and Stoneman were riding south on their doomed mission, Howard and his Army of the Tennessee had stretched themselves toward the railroad at East Point about as far as they safely could. Sherman planned to extend his southward advance by drawing Schofield's army east of the city, swinging it around behind Thomas as Howard's had done, and pushing it south, extending his army group's right flank.

The Army of the Ohio began its maneuver on August 1. The next day, Schofield had marched far enough to extend Sherman's right another mile and a half, almost to Utoy Creek, an estuary flowing westward maybe two miles south of the Lick Skillet road.

Atlanta doesn't have many Civil War earthworks, especially inside the I-285 perimeter highway. But here they are, a Confederate artillery emplacement with rifle pits off Cascade Road. The site is in Cascade Springs Nature Preserve, a woodlands park owned by the City of Atlanta. (ahc)

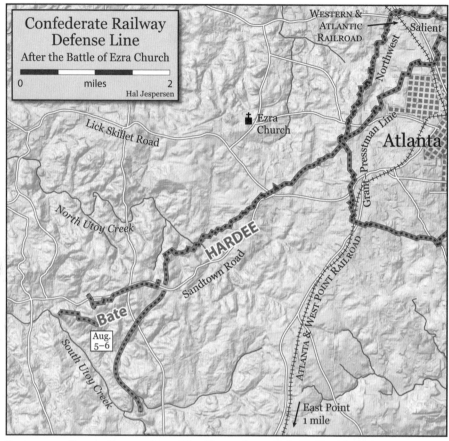

CONFEDERATE RAILWAY DEFENSE LINE—After his repulse on July 28, Hood had his troops extend fortifications southwest of the city to fend off Sherman's march to cut the Macon & Western and Atlanta & West Point Railroads. The two lines diverged at East Point.

Confederate cavalry resisted the Yankees' advance while Hood's infantry dug a line of fortifications to protect the railroad running out of Atlanta. After his withdrawal from the battlefield of Ezra Church, S. D. Lee positioned his troops west of the Grant-Presstman perimeter about a mile and a half north of the railway. Beginning on the night of July 29, Lee had his men start digging a line of entrenchments to protect the locomotive route. This "railway defense line," constructed in the first half of August, eventually extended a half-dozen miles southwest of the city, featuring head-logged earthworks, palisades, abatis, and cleared fields of fire.

"The work of intrenching was pushed forward with vigor night and day," recorded Maj. Gen. Patton Anderson, brought from Florida to take command of John C. Brown's division,

"till a feeling of security and even defiance pervaded the whole line." Behind the front line were traverses and zig-zags for the supporting troops. "The ground in rear of our works," wrote General Manigault, "was completely honeycombed."

In August, the key tactical front was thus no longer along the Grant-Presstman perimeter of fortifications surrounding Atlanta, but the railway defense line extending from it southwest of the city. As Sherman gradually extended his lines, hoping to be able to turn Hood's left—as he had done so many times against Johnston— he found the Rebels invariably entrenched before him. Sherman begrudgingly paid compliment to his adversary's industry. Hood, he telegraphed Grant on August 4, "shows a bold front wherever I get at him."

To help man the newly extended fortifications, Bate's division of Hardee's corps was brought out from the city toward Utoy Creek, taking position at one point on high ground in a salient out in front of the railway defense line and digging in.

Sherman was becoming impatient. He was compelled to realize that he would not be able to reach beyond the Rebels' flank, so he began thinking of an infantry sortie against their

After the battle of Ezra Church, Hood's troops dug a long line of entrenchments southwest from Atlanta to protect the railroad running to East Point. At this point, near Utoy Creek, some four miles outside the Confederates' perimeter of fortifications around the city, Maj. Gen. William Bate's division held the Southern works. Sherman extended his lines, as well, and on August 4 ordered Schofield with his XXII Corps, supported by John Palmer's XIV Corps of Thomas's army, to "move directly on the railroad." "If necessary to secure this end," he barked, "ordinary parapets must be charged and carried." Squabbling between Palmer and Schofield over seniority prevented anything more than a strong reconnaissance against the Rebel works on the 5th. On the morning of August 6, Col. James Reilly's brigade (Cox's division, XXIII Corps) sallied against Bate's line and was bloodily repulsed. (ahc)

Confederate Maj. Gen. William B. Bate, born in Bledsoe's Lick, Tennessee in 1826, had little formal education but became a journalist, lawyer, attorney general and state legislator. Enlisting as a private at the start of the war, Bate was elected colonel of the 2nd Tennessee. As brigadier (October 1862) and major general (February 1864), he fought in all of the Army of Tennessee's campaigns. (lphcw)

very line. On August 4, he directed Schofield to "move directly on the railroad," not halting till he had "absolute control of it." "Ordinary parapets must be charged and carried," he wrote, if the Federals were to gain the East Point road. In addition to his own XXIII Corps, Sherman directed that Maj. Gen. John Palmer's XIV Corps of Thomas's army was to cooperate with Schofield in the advance.

That was the hitch. When Schofield issued orders for the advance, Palmer refused to obey them, egotistically claiming he would not take orders from an officer of lesser seniority, which Schofield was. Sherman interceded but could not change Palmer's mind, whereupon the XIV Corps commander submitted his resignation. At Sherman's recommendation, Jefferson C. Davis was to be promoted to major general and given command of the corps.

By the time Schofield finally launched his reconnaissance-in-force against Bate's line in the "battle" of Utoy Creek, August 6, the Southerners had strengthened their trenches with abatis. The Federals had heard the Rebels chopping away at trees, and thus when Col. James Reilly's brigade of Cox's division advanced, the Northerners were not surprised when they ran into, as Cox said, "an entanglement of the undergrowth, half cut off, bent down, and interlaced." The obstacles helped Bate's troops easily break the assault. The Federals were repulsed with losses of 76 killed and 199 wounded, plus 31 men captured when they actually managed to get near the enemy parapet. Bate's casualties amounted to a mere 15 or 20 men.

The next day, units of the XIV Corps sortied against Bate again. This time they overran the Rebel picket line and rounded up

200 prisoners. But they lost twice as many men in the effort. When the enemy began to maneuver around his left, Bate withdrew back into the main railway defense line.

The historian at this point must push his armchair back. Utoy Creek was the fifth site of a frontal assault called for by Sherman. It followed Resaca on May 14-15, New Hope Church on May 25, Pickett's Mill on May 27, and Kennesaw Mountain on June 27. In every case, as to be expected, Union infantry attacking an entrenched enemy position was repulsed. The irony is that Sherman's historical reputation in the literature of the Atlanta campaign is that of an artful maneuverer. Hood's reputation is that of a futile frontal attacker, even though we have seen that on July 22 and July 28, he envisioned assaults upon the enemy flank, not front. After a century and a half, the literature has yet to catch up on this point.

The setback at Utoy Creek taught Sherman the danger of underestimating his enemy. "The parapets of Atlanta present a well-filled line wherever we approach them," he wrote Grant. On August 7, he telegraphed Halleck that he could not again assail the Rebels' entrenched works. Nor could he extend his lines, which then ran approximately seven or eight miles from northeast of the city to its southwest.

While he pondered his next move, Sherman settled for having his artillery to keep firing shot and shell into Atlanta.

The uninformed hiker gazing from the pathways in the Cascade Springs Nature Preserve may not recognize there earthen features as Civil War fortifications. (The park signage makes no mention of them.) They are on the high ground overlooking the spring below. However, back in August 1864, there would have been no mistaking them. For several days before the Union infantry advanced against Bate's line, Southerners entrenched and constructed abatis as well as entanglements of underbrush and logs. Federals heard the ominous "constant chopping and falling of trees," as one recorded, which foretold a hard time ahead for any attackers. (ahc)

"Too Hot to Be Endured"

CHAPTER TEN

As commander of the XV Corps in Grant's army during the Vicksburg Campaign, Sherman had learned much from his mentor, especially how an army severed from its base of supply could live off the land while pushing deep into central Mississippi. Then, as the Federals besieged Vicksburg, eventually forcing Confederate Lt. Gen. John C. Pemberton to surrender, Sherman had also witnessed Grant's artillery bombardment of the city.

After Grant's capture of the fortress, Sherman had marched a small army east from Vicksburg against Joe Johnston's forces, pushing them back to Jackson. There in mid-July, Sherman laid semi-siege to the city, ordering his artillery to bombard it while his infantry sortied against the Rebel works and his cavalry rode around their flanks, threatening their supply line. Sherman boasted that his cannonade would "make the town too hot" for Johnston. Eventually the Confederates abandoned Jackson (for the second time), but it is questionable whether the Federal shelling of the city was a significant factor in their evacuation.

A year later, as his forces laid semi-siege to

The only tourists to downtown Atlanta today are conventioneers and sports fans for games at the Georgia Dome and other venues. Motorists drive over the area of the city's wartime railroad, which George Barnard photographed in fall 1864. After the war, the city built viaducts over the railroad yards. In Atlanta's early days, the chugging of trains through downtown held up passengers and business traffic alike. (ahc)

"Almost every house has what we call a 'gopher hole' attached to it," observed Capt. Alfred Hough of the 19th U. S. Infantry, just one Federal noticing all the bombproofs which civilians had dug during the bombardment. The building behind this one has been identified as the Charles E. Grenville Flour Mill in the southwest suburbs. (loc)

While Sherman's rifled guns bombarded the city, shorter-range smoothbores occasionally pummeled the Rebels in their fortified lines. Confederates dug a casemate there perhaps as much for shelter from the summer sun as from Yankee shells. During the occupation, Barnard photographed Northern soldiers lolling about in a Rebel fort west of the city. With no threat of enemy attack, sentries sit atop the parapet. A bored soldier reads in the dugout to kill time. (loc)

Atlanta, Sherman again called for his rifled artillery to throw shot and shell into downtown. After Utoy Creek, with his army group's lines stretched to their utmost, the Northern commander intensified his cannonade. "I do not deem it prudent to extend more to the right," he wrote Halleck on August 7, "but will push forward daily by parallels, and make the inside of Atlanta too hot to be endured."

Again, it is questionable whether Sherman thought an artillery bombardment of downtown Atlanta would force his enemy to abandon the place, especially since that enemy was no longer Joe Johnston, but J. B. Hood. Still, Sherman seemed to take a personal interest in the cannonade when he ordered it to be intensified. "I would like to get a good battery as near it as possible that will reach the heart of Atlanta," he wrote on August 8, "and reduce it to ruins." Instead of directing his artillerymen to aim for the train depot at the center of the city, where

the Rebels' supplies were unloaded, Sherman wanted a general leveling of the downtown area as a whole. "Let us destroy Atlanta and make it a desolation," he wrote to Howard.

Accordingly, Sherman sent for heavier guns that could lob 30-pound explosive shells deep into the city. When they had not arrived by August 9, Sherman ordered a huge bombardment anyway: all of his hundred rifled cannon to fire 50 rounds each into the city. They did so, resulting in 5,000 shells hurled into downtown on that single day.

There is evidence that Thomas, whose artillery north of town kept up much of Sherman's shelling, knew the location of Hood's headquarters and directed his guns to aim for them. A Northern spy slipping in and out of the city on August 3 reported that the enemy HQ was on Whitehall Street near Rodgers Tannery. A few days later, expecting the big guns from Chattanooga, Thomas informed Sherman that he had chosen a position

If Sherman had any target for his cannon bombarding downtown, it should have been the big passenger depot, the "car shed" in the middle of the city. It received so few hits, however, that it was standing remarkably undamaged at the end of the shelling. Barnard photographed it here in early November, just as Union supply officers were packing goods on northbound trains before Sherman's forces struck out across Georgia in their march to the sea. Magnification of the dray in the mid-ground shows a handbill tacked to it advertising a downtown concert on November 8. (loc)

Pvt. James Snell of the 52nd Illinois observed that the Federals' artillery fire "did great damage to the place, riddling and tearing down houses, and burning others to the ground." George Barnard took this picture of the remains of a house destroyed by Northern shells. (loc)

Charles Todd Quintard (1824-1898) was born in Connecticut, schooled in New York City, and graduated in 1846 to become a physician. He moved south, married, and in Memphis decided to join the Episcopal ministry. After ordination as priest, he tended to parishes in Nashville. At the start of the War, Quintard joined the 1st Tennessee as chaplain. During the Atlanta Campaign, he served as chaplain at large for the Army of Tennessee. On August 9, 1864, he accompanied Bishop Henry Lay to Hood's headquarters. During their visit, Yankee cannon started shelling the area. Quintard was unsettled, but seeing the nonchalance of Hood and his staff, "I concluded that everything was going on all right according to the art of war," he later wrote, "and we stood it with the best of them." (loc)

The Right Reverend Henry C. Lay, Episcopal bishop of Arkansas, happened to be in Atlanta staying with friends when the Northern shells started falling on the city, July 20. On August 9, a heavy day of shelling, Bishop Lay was at General Hood's headquarters. "Shells are exploding all around Head Qrs," he recorded in his diary, "and it is proposed to move them." Soon afterward, Hood and his staff moved their headquarters farther out into the southwest suburbs, which were less frequently shelled by the Yankees. (loc)

Solomon Luckie is probably antebellum Atlanta's best-known free African-American. The 1859 city directory lists his barbershop in the Atlanta Hotel. In August 1864, Luckie was standing at the corner of Whitehall and Alabama Streets when a Northern shell struck a lamppost, sending an iron fragment into his leg. Bystanders rushed him to the nearby hospital, but physicians could not save him. His burial place is today unknown. (ahc)

for them which "enfilades White Hall street, upon which is General Hood's headquarters."

In the big bombardment of August 9, Hood and his staff indeed came under cannonfire. Two Episcopal clergymen were visiting Hood's offices when the Yankee missiles started falling. "Hood's quarters came in for a large share of the shelling," Bishop Henry Lay recorded. "Some of the shells fell very thickly about the General's headquarters," Chaplain Charles Quintard entered into his diary that day. Quintard worried about the "unhealthy" setting, but when he and Bishop Lay saw that "the General and his staff did not seem in the least disturbed" by the cannonade, they determined to stick it out too.

Hood and his officers were not injured by the Northern projectiles, but a number of Atlanta's civilians were. A shell that struck Mrs. John Weaver's house on Walton Street July 23 wounded her and killed her child. A shell killed Francis Hale, workman in the Western & Atlantic woodshop, on August 17. Probably the most famous cannon casualties were Joseph F. Warner and his 9-year-old daughter Elizabeth, who were killed by a shell on the night of August 3. The story of their deaths was so talked about that even the *New York Tribune* printed a long article on it.

We will never know exactly how many non-combatants met their death by Sherman's shells, but the accepted estimate is about a score of civilians. Based on typical casualty rates, that would lead to a guess of times-two or times-three wounded before the Yankee bombardment ended on August 25.

George Barnard titled this photograph "Near the foot of Whitehall Street, Atlanta." The "Auction & Negro Sales" sign is for the firm that advertised itself in the Atlanta Southern Confederacy in May 1863 as "Crawford, Frazer & Co., General Commission Merchants, Auctioneers and Dealers in Negroes, No. 8 Whitehall St." (loc)

Today, the stretch of Whitehall Street south of Peachtree is the site of the Five Points station for Metropolitan Atlanta Rapid Transit Authority (MARTA). The historic downtown intersection of Whitehall, Peachtree, Marietta, and Decatur Streets was referred to as "Five Points" in Margaret Mitchell's novel *Gone With the Wind* (1936). Subsequent researchers, however, have shown the urban nickname did not come about till 1904 or 1905, so dubbed by Walter Taylor, editor of the *Atlanta Journal*. (ahc)

Wheeler's Raid and Kilpatrick's Raid

CHAPTER ELEVEN

"The large force sent from Chattanooga prevented our working at the tunnel," Confederate Maj. Gen. Joseph Wheeler reported during his cavalry raid into north Georgia behind Sherman's lines in mid-August 1864. Actually, given the technology of the time (no dynamite or power drilling tools), Southerners would not have been able to destroy the railroad tunnel cut through Chetoogeta Mountain, no matter how much time they might have had. (dd)

When Hood was promoted general and made commander of the Army of Tennessee, Confederate Secretary of War James A. Seddon had telegraphed him, expressing the government's hopes that he would "cut the communication of the enemy." Defeat of McCook's and Stoneman's raiders encouraged Hood to indulge the War Department in its suggestion. Hood determined to send "Fighting Joe" Wheeler's cavalry on a raid behind Sherman's lines, to strike at and cut the Yankees' single-track railroad bringing their supplies from Chattanooga.

Just to be sure, Hood wrote President Davis on August 2, offering the proposal that "since our late success over the enemy's cavalry, I hope now to be able, by interrupting Sherman's communications, either to force him to fight me in position or to retreat."

The president gave his approval. Hood would detach Wheeler and roughly half of the army's cavalry—4,500 or 5,000 horsemen—for the raid. He ordered 600 pounds of blasting powder and 2,000 feet of fuse to be brought from Augusta and Macon—indications Hood hoped

In recent years, the Georgia Historical Society, based in Savannah, has been placing historical markers around the state. This one in Dalton states that when Wheeler approached on August 14, "the 14th United States Colored Troops (USCT), whose enlisted men were mostly former slaves, helped drive off a Confederate cavalry attack on the Western and Atlantic Railroad, U. S. General William T. Sherman's main supply line during the Atlanta Campaign." (dd)

his cavalry would use them in blowing up bridges or tunnels along Sherman's vital W&A supply line.

Hood was careful to retain more than half of his mounted forces. On August 10, the day Wheeler set out on his raid, returns showed fully 12,800 officers and men in the army's cavalry corps.

Wheeler and his troopers set out way east of Atlanta, near Covington—the farthest point on the Georgia Railroad to which the blasting powder could be carried by rail from the Augusta powder works. Riding northwest, they came upon the Western & Atlantic at Big Shanty (today's Kennesaw) and pried up a mile of track. Near Calhoun the next day, they captured a herd of a thousand cattle and sent them back to Hood's army. A few more miles of track were torn up north of Resaca. On August 14, the Confederates captured Dalton and burned three trains loaded with supplies.

Northwest of Dalton, a long railroad tunnel runs through Chetoogeta Mountain, which may have been the reason Wheeler brought blasting powder. But several thousand enemy troops were approaching, and the Southerners could not damage the underpass. "The large force sent from Chattanooga prevented our

The CSX Railroad runs through Kennesaw, Georgia, today, just as the Western & Atlantic ran through Big Shanty in 1864. Back then, a mixed passenger and freight train took two hours to run from Atlanta's Car Shed to Big Shanty station, with a stop at Marietta. (ahc)

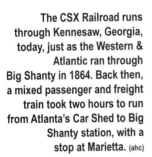

working at the tunnel," Wheeler reported on the 16th. The Confederates wrecked another half-mile of track before they rode off. Wheeler led them not toward Chattanooga and Nashville, which was the main railroad route used to bring Sherman his supplies, but northeast, in the direction of Knoxville.

In Atlanta, Hood had no sure source of information on what Wheeler was able to do in north Georgia. Rumors swirled. "Railroad in enemy's rear reported to be badly torn up," Shoup entered in his journal. On the 18th, he recorded, "prisoners report the tunnel blown up by Wheeler, captured Dalton and Resaca, burned Etowah bridge, and are going up the railroad."

Only a smidgen of this hearsay, however, was true. Actually, Wheeler's railroad damage was so minimal, and Sherman's railroad work crews were so efficient, that the Western & Atlantic between Big Shanty and Chattanooga was completely repaired by August 18.

In terms of achieving Hood's objective, Wheeler's raid was already a failure.

*   *   *

Far from affecting the outcome of the campaign, Wheeler's cavalry raid had barely inconvenienced Sherman and his army group outside of Atlanta. "Wheeler," he wrote, "may hurt some of the minor points, but, on the whole East Tennessee is a good place for him to break down his horses, and a poor place to steal new ones."

Nevertheless, Wheeler's departure caused Sherman to consider sending another mounted force against the Macon & Western, despite the failure of the McCook-Stoneman raid. "Wheeler is out of the way," he reasoned; "when

"Big Shanty," now Kennesaw, Georgia. The town's name developed from the shanties built here for railroad workers during construction of the Western & Atlantic, 1838-1841. The area, at higher elevation, came to be called "the big grade to the shanties," and eventually to Big Shanty. It was here, on the morning of April 12, 1862, that James J. Andrews and nineteen volunteers from Ohio regiments boarded the northbound locomotive and several boxcars, launching a raid to break the railroad and cut telegraph lines to Chattanooga. After Southerners set out in pursuit, the exploit has been dubbed "the Great Locomotive Chase." (ahc)

Theodore R. Davis drew this sketch of Big Shanty depot for *Harper's Weekly*. Maj. Gen. Joe Wheeler and 4,500 mounted troops set out on a raid behind Sherman's lines on August 10. "Gen. Wheeler commenced destroying the railroad at Big Shanty last Friday night [August 12]," crowed a Georgia newspaper, "and has continued the destruction from Big Shanty to Chattanooga." In reality, Wheeler reported that his men wrecked the railroad at Big Shanty for a length of all of one mile. (hw)

Lovejoy's Station, six miles south of Jonesboro, was the target of Federal cavalry in late July when Ed McCook's division rode in to wreck a couple of miles of track. In his raid of August 18-22, Judson Kilpatrick's objective was not Lovejoy's, but Jonesboro. Nevertheless, Kilpatrick returned to Lovejoy's Station at the start of Sherman's march to the sea in mid-November 1864. His division, on the right flank of Federal infantry marching out of Atlanta, clashed with Rebel horsemen here on November 16. (ahc)

shall we use cavalry if not now?" Stoneman was a prisoner, and both his and McCook's divisions were wrecked, but Kenner Garrard's and Judson Kilpatrick's divisions were in good shape. Sherman did not hold Garrard in high regard: "if he can see a horseman in the distance with a spyglass he will turn back."

Kilpatrick, on the other hand, had shown more initiative. "With his own and Garrard's cavalry," Sherman wrote Thomas, Kilpatrick "could ride right around Atlanta and smash the Macon road all to pieces." In his orders for the raid, Sherman told his cavalry leader to head for Jonesboro, a M&W depot two dozen miles south of Atlanta, according to the railroad's own measurement.

Promising to inflict significant damage on the enemy's railroad, Kilpatrick began his raid late on August 18, riding southwest from Atlanta with 4,700 troopers. Brigadier General Lawrence S. "Sul" Ross's brigade of Texas cavalry, numbering merely 400, could only keep Hood's headquarters informed of the Yankees' progress. The M&W was clearly their objective, but Hood could not pinpoint precisely where they were headed. He sent alerts to posts along the line south of Atlanta, and dispatched an infantry brigade to reinforce Frank Armstrong's cavalry at Jonesboro.

But Armstrong moved south to Lovejoy's Station just as Kilpatrick's column rode into Jonesboro on the afternoon of August 19. It was raining and the Federals could not start fires to burn crossties and bend rails, so they simply pried them up for five hours. Then, around 10 p.m., Kilpatrick ordered his men to mount up for the ride back. After a brief run-in with some Rebels, they reentered Sherman's lines at Decatur on the 22nd.

Kilpatrick reported some 200 men lost in his foray, in which he claimed he had knocked out the enemy rail line for 10 days. Actually, it was only for two. Striding into Sherman's headquarters, Kilpatrick proudly announced his achievement—only to have the commanding general point out the sound of train whistles from Rebel locomotives chugging into Atlanta from Macon.

Frank Crawford Armstrong (1835-1909) had served in the U. S. dragoons before the war and actually led a company of them at First Manassas before resigning from the U. S. army. He then fought out in Missouri and Arkansas, gaining his colonelcy in May 1862. Promoted brigadier in spring 1863, Armstrong led a cavalry brigade under Forrest and eventually William H. Jackson, with whose division he joined Johnston's army in May 1864. (nf)

East of Lovejoy's, Sul Ross's Texans dismounted and formed line, buttressed by Capt. Edward Croft's Georgia Battery. A table at Nash Farm relates the action of a 12-pounder howitzer commanded by Lt. George Young. (nf)

Hood Tries to Make Good his Losses

CHAPTER TWELVE

When John B. Hood took command of the Army of Tennessee, it numbered about 59,000 officers and men present for duty in all three services (official returns dated July 10 give the precise figure of 59,196). The next report, dated July 31, was tallied after Hood's three battles that month. Confederate casualties on July 20, 22, and 28 totaled about 10,800 men.

Thus, to see the army numbering 48,396 soldiers at the end of July seems remarkable. More so still was its strength in returns for August 10, which actually gave a numerical increase, if only a slight one: 51,946 infantry, cavalry and artillery present for duty.

One can only understand these numbers by remembering how General Hood took a number of steps to strengthen his army.

He called for medical directors of army hospitals to scour the wards and identify convalescents well enough to return to the field. Newspapers carried stories of Hood personally strolling through hospitals looking for shirkers. The accounts were untrue, but they made for good press. A Macon paper reported the number of sick and wounded soldiers in the

General Hood's efforts to beef up his ranks in early August 1864 included sending soldiers detailed as cooks and clerks to the front lines to take up a musket. He even called upon "supernumerary" cannoneers. "He has ordered the arming of every artillerist, except from number one to six, who are absolutely necessary to handle a piece," observed one newspaper account. "This order converting artillery into infantry caused considerable fluttering among the battery boys" (*Augusta Chronicle & Sentinel*, Aug. 12, 1864). (jm)

Incessant skirmishing and cannonading brought casualties on both sides even without a big battle. On August 19, Maj. Gen. Grenville Dodge, XVI Corps commander (above), was seriously wounded in his lines west of Atlanta. That same day, Union Brig. Gen. Joseph Lightburn also suffered a wound, albeit a slighter one to the head. (loc)

city had dropped because of "the stringent orders of Gen. Hood to forward every man able for duty."

Men who had secured non-combat positions were ordered to the front. This meant hospital stewards, clerks, couriers, and cooks whose places could be filled by disabled soldiers, even women or slaves. Merely cutting the number of clerks in the army's commissary and other departments, one Confederate wrote approvingly, "returned many men to the ranks." One newspaper column highlighted "the number of new men returned from the cooking detachments" in Clayton's division alone—some three hundred, enough for a "good regiment."

An army with a lot of wagons uses a lot of teamsters, and Hood determined to give those suitable for soldiering a musket and a place in the trenches. Hood's inspector general called for slaveowners to hire out their bondsman for $25 a month, with food and clothing to be provided by the army. Advertisements went out for 1,500 Negroes. "Gen. Hood has placed a gun in the hands of all his wagoners, and wants to place the wagon whip in the hands of darkies," reported one newspaper. Agents travelled to cities around the state to draw up contracts with owners. The Augusta *Chronicle & Sentinel* predicted such efforts could bring 3,000 previously detailed men to the front lines, but the number was probably closer to a thousand.

The commanding general even reduced each cannon crew to bring forth a rifle-toter. Gun crews of the time consisted of seven men; Hood called for one of them to leave the artillery service and join the infantry. This order caused "considerable fluttering among the artillery boys," according to one source.

Hood was well aware of many soldiers absent from his army without leave. He asked that the press publicize his appeal for their return. It did. "Absentees to the Front!" cried the *Macon Telegraph*. "Return to Your Colors," exclaimed the *Columbus Times*. Voluntarism, of course, would only go so far, so Hood urged conscript officers around the state to search more stringently for men without documents of exemption and to send them to the front.

As a further manpower measure, Hood asked the authorities in Richmond to spread word in other theaters, as far away as the Trans-Mississippi, that soldiers AWOL would be granted pardon if they but returned to their commands.

Altogether these efforts added at least a few thousand men to Hood's army. General Bragg exaggerated when he wrote President Davis that "the increase by arrival of extra duty men and convalescents, &c., is about 5,000." But any increase helped after the costly battles of July. Captain J. B. Jordan of the 36th Alabama told Union interrogators in mid-August that his Company G had numbered 14 men at Kennesaw, had received 12 replacements since the battle of July 22, and by August 13 mustered 34 muskets.

Not to be overlooked were the Georgia Militia, who numbered about 2,000 in mid-July. The militiamen were often derided, but Hood considered them useful in manning the fortifications of the city. He therefore worked with Governor Joseph E. Brown to bring forth more "mellish," and in a few weeks had 5,000 of them under Major General Smith. The veterans liked to poke fun at the old men and boys, but they appreciated their presence nonetheless. A Confederate officer of engineers recorded this story in his journal, dated August 24:

> *Some few of what soldiers call "new issue" joined us today. These are persons who have been called into service by recent proclamations and orders, most of them never having served in the army before. Unfortunately for them, they were marched along in a body through the camps of some of the older troops and consequently were made the target for innumerable jests and jibes. I remember one rather delicate-looking young man who seemed to attract an unusual share of this kind of attention. He was much more neatly dressed than his companions and had on what was exceedingly unusual at this time, a clean shirt and white collar. He had also a white pocket-handkerchief, which he would*

In his efforts to strengthen his army after the battles of July 20-28, Hood called for medical officers to screen for skulkers. The *Macon Telegraph* ran a column about a Confederate surgeon in the city who went through a bunch of sick-leave applicants, dismissing their protestations of ill health. To one who asked for continued hospitalization, the surgeon rejoined, "Going to the country a little while, and perchance killing a Yankee will do you more good than anything else. Fall in." (jm)

occasionally flourish as he passed along. One fellow asked him if he did not wish to "trade off his old clothes when they put him in uniform." Presently, an old, dirty, ragged Tennesseean hailed him with something like the following: "I say, mister, what do you do with that 'ar white rag yer toting in yer hand?" "New issue" halted and, turning upon his interrogator a look of fierce scorn, replied, "I use this to wipe my face on. If you had it you'd hoist it on your ramrod!" (The hoisting of a white handkerchief on a ramrod was a kind of truce, begging the opposite picket not to fire.) The soldiers laughed and "melish" passed on without further molestation.

Brig. Gen. Thomas E. G. Ransom was serving in Louisiana in the spring of 1864 when he took a serious knee wound at Mansfield on April 8. Upon recovery he joined Sherman's forces at Atlanta, taking charge of a division in the XVI Corps. After Grenville Dodge was sent home from his wounding August 19, General Ransom succeeded him in command of the corps. (loc)

"Our Army has been strengthened by the Militia," Lt. Andrew J. Neal of Perry's Florida Battery wrote to his sister on August 4. Even more did Neal appreciate Hood's work to strengthen the army: "all the bands cook details extra artillery men drivers and dead heads have been brought to the front and given muskets."

*   *   *

For their part, Hood's troops remained as defiant as ever, yet Hood was content with the status quo: so long as the enemy were not pushing to cut the Macon railroad, he was holding Sherman at bay and keeping his army at least marginally subsisted. Sherman, with his lines fully extended, having concluded he had no probability of flanking the Rebel army, and seemingly satisfied with this bombardment of downtown Atlanta, in mid-August pursued no new aggressive initiative. Brigadier General Francis A. Shoup, Hood's chief of staff, recorded in his daily journal "no change in our lines" and

Indiana-born Francis Asbury Shoup graduated from West Point in 1855 and was stationed in Florida. Resigning from the army just before the war, he received a Confederate artillery lieutenant's commission. At Shiloh he served as Hardee's chief of artillery; afterward Beauregard appointed him to be his artillery chief. In April 1864 Shoup reported to General Johnston as the Army of Tennessee's chief of artillery. After General Mackall's departure as the army's chief of staff, Hood named Shoup to take the job. Following the war General Shoup became an Episcopal priest, and was photographed as such here. (phcw)

"all quiet along our lines" 11 times in the period of August 12-24.

The men in the trenches sensed the lull and lapsed into the fraternizing that often occurred during the American Civil War. "Our boys got to hollowing over to them," wrote one Illinois soldier on August 11, "and the two parties for the first time at this place, quit shooting and entered into conversation." A Wisconsin private wrote home about one such instance of fraternization. "We had two visitors day before yesterday. They were Johnny Rebs," he explained.

They came over and took dinner with us and brought over some corn bread and tobacco and we made some coffee and all sat down on the ground together and had a good chat as well as a good dinner. They gave us some tobacco and we gave them some coffee to take back with them. . . . If they would let the soldiers settle this thing it would not be long before we would be on terms of peace.

Inevitably the officers heard of this camaraderie and ordered it to stop. The sound of muskets and cannon firing provided evidence that there was still a war very much going on, as further attested by the attendant casualties. "It is a picket fight all the time," observed William B. Honnell of Mississippi, "we lose some men every day in our brigade either killed or wounded."

Losses included even the brass. On August 10, Major General Bate caught a minie ball in the knee that put him out of service for two months. When he returned to the army, he held his crutch rather than his sword when riding among and cheering his men. On the 19th, Major General Dodge was struck in the head by a rifle ball that knocked him out with a concussion. He was eventually sent home and never returned to Sherman's army. Brigadier General Thomas E. G. Ransom succeeded him in command of the XVI Corps.

After the battle of Seven Pines, Gustavus W. Smith did not hold an important command until Georgia Governor Joseph E. Brown appointed him major general of his state militia in early June 1864. At the height of the crisis, with Sherman outside of Atlanta, Smith commanded about 5,000 old men and boys. "The Georgia militia were good fighters," Smith later boasted, and even Gen. Hood recognized their value manning the fortifications of Atlanta. (loc)

Sherman's "Grand Movement by the Right Flank"

CHAPTER THIRTEEN

Warren House. One of the landmarks of the Jonesboro battlefield is the house of Guy L. Warren, one of the town's first commissioners, built in 1840. During the battle, Southerners used it for a field hospital until the 52nd Illinois occupied it on September 2. Union surgeons used it as a hospital, as well. The Warren house, at 102 W. Mimosa Drive and Main Street north of downtown, is today available for tours and special events. (hp)

Upon the realization that Kilpatrick and his cavalry in their Jonesboro raid of August 18-22 had not cut the Macon & Western, Sherman determined to "make the matter certain." He would lead most of his army—fully six of his seven infantry corps—in a wide march south of Atlanta, swinging southeast to "try the Macon road," he wired General Halleck, "without which Hood cannot feed his army." Slocum's XX Corps would withdraw back to the Chattahoochee at the railroad bridge, guarding it and threatening Atlanta from afar. Hood would be forced to stretch his already overstretched army both to defend Atlanta and somehow parry Sherman's massive lunge at the southward railroad. Orders for the big maneuver, which he called "the grand movement by the right flank," went out August 23.

The Federals withdrew from their lines gradually. On the night of August 25-26,

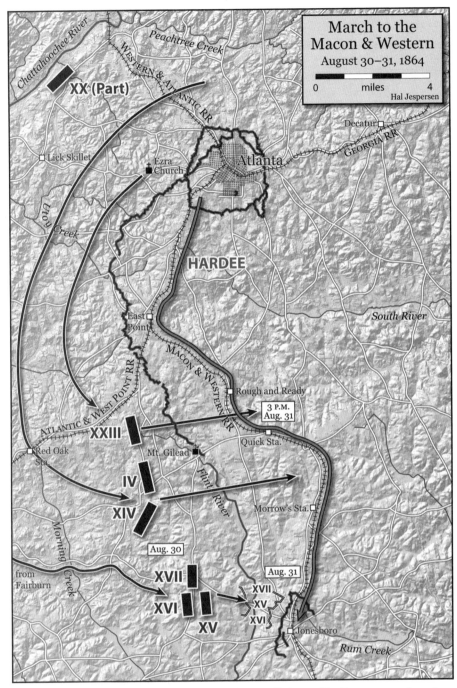

MARCH TO THE MACON & WESTERN—The approach of Howard's Army of the Tennessee on Jonesboro occupied Hood's attention August 30-31, but it was actually Schofield's and Thomas's infantry which cut the vital railroad on the afternoon of August 31.

the IV Corps, Thomas's farthest left, fell back and headed west as the XX withdrew toward the Chattahoochee. Howard's three corps, plus the XIV, started moving the next night. Last to withdraw from its lines west of the city was the XXIII, which began its march midday on the 28th.

Confederates knew quickly from the sound of wagons and artillery that the enemy was on the move. Pickets probing at dawn on August 26 found trenches north of the city empty and the Yankees gone from that sector. "General Hood and his Chief of Staff 'Shoup' are in high glee," Lieutenant Trask entered in his journal, "they think that he is preparing to retreat." Failure of Union artillery to open fire that morning seemed to confirm HQ's first impression.

But several hours later, Confederates west of the Western & Atlantic found Yankees still in their front. Hood ordered Red Jackson to send out patrols to find the enemy's new position. At nightfall, Hood wired Richmond that the enemy left had withdrawn, but his right south of the railroad remained in place.

The next day Southerners learned of the further disappearance of Yankees west of town. General French sent a recon force toward the Chattahoochee and encountered the enemy; prisoners identified themselves as from the XX Corps.

On the afternoon of August 27, cavalry reports came in that the Federal infantry was marching southwest, seven miles from Atlanta. Hood sent Frank Armstrong's horsemen to stay in front of the Union

After ripping up the A&WP Railroad along the five-mile stretch from Red Oak to Fairburn on August 29, Sherman sent his six infantry corps on a march southeast toward the Macon & Western. Brig. Gen. Jeff Davis's XIV Corps struck out from Red Oak (halfway between East Point and Fairburn) and at nightfall of the 30th encamped in the area of Shoal Creek Church, four miles southeast of Red Oak. The Macon railroad at Morrow's Station lay about the same distance ahead. (ahc)

column and harass it. That evening, he informed Secretary Seddon of the enemy movement, even though he had to concede "the exact intention of the enemy has not yet been ascertained."

Yet clearly Sherman was headed for the railroad. Even the press picked this up. The Memphis/Atlanta *Appeal,* the last paper left in the city, reported that the enemy was in motion toward the West Point and Macon rail lines. Sherman's obvious intent was to cut the M&W, but precisely where, Hood could not predict.

East Point? On the 28th, Bate's division was sent there to reinforce Cleburne's.

Rough and Ready, three-and-a-half miles farther? Several brigades of Brown's division went there.

All the way to Jonesboro, 10 miles more to the south? Two brigades were moved to that point, as well.

Meanwhile, Armstrong's and Sul Ross's cavalry kept watch on the Yankees, reporting them as having stopped at the Atlantic & West Point (A&WP) rail line. "Yankees have not left West Point railroad," Hood telegraphed that night.

The railroad from Atlanta through West Point to Montgomery was barely back in operation, repaired from the damage wreaked by Rousseau's cavalry near Opelika and Auburn. Even though speed would have been an asset in his "grand movement"—by fast marching the Federal advance might have reached the Macon railroad, his true objective—Sherman nonetheless ordered his infantry to halt and set to work tearing up the A&WP This they did throughout August 29. Cump never tired of lecturing his officers and men on the art of railroad demolition: "Let the destruction be so thorough that not a rail or tie can be used again."

The Yankees performed their destruction in ways their commander would have liked. As Logan's troops threw dirt to fill track-cuts, they also planted percussion shells to explode against any Rebel repair crews. Up to 12.5 miles of railway were wrecked. Armstrong's and Jackson's troopers could do nothing but watch.

Sherman's decision to hold his columns on the railroad between Fairburn and Red Oak allowed Hood to fix the enemy's position. On August 29, General Hardee, in command at East Point, was called to headquarters for an evening conference about the situation. "We know that five certainly, perhaps six Corps are on the West Point R. Road," the general wrote his wife the next morning. Hardee was spot-on. The Federal IV, XIV, XV, XVI, and XVII corps were all at work prying up rails; the XXIII, last to have left Atlanta, was catching up.

But again, after they left the A&WP, where were the Yankees going? Shoup, the chief of staff, entered in his journal that Jonesboro and Rough and Ready were the enemy's probable objectives. Hood therefore kept shifting troops to his left, such as Patton Anderson's division to East Point. "The general commanding, in his opinion," Shoup recorded, "has taken all necessary precautions, and made such disposition of his forces as to prevent either of the above-named places [Rough and Ready, Jonesboro] from falling into the enemy's hands." Hardee

An unlikely Confederate hero in the battle of Jonesboro was Fr. Emmeran Bliemel, chaplain of the 10th Tennessee. As the Southern attack faltered on the afternoon of August 31, Father Bliemel was tending to wounded soldiers on the battlefield when a shell struck, decapitating him. This monument, dedicated by the local Knights of Columbus, stands on the grounds of the Clayton County courthouse in Jonesboro. (hp)

Old Red Oak Post Office, southwest of Atlanta. "Aug. 30, the move E. against the Macon R.R. began," states this historical marker seven miles southwest of East Point. (The latter town was the eastern terminus of the railroad almost to the Chattahoochee above Columbus, which ended aptly enough at "West Point.") "Siege operations on the Atlanta front having failed," the marker states, Sherman was swinging most of his army away from the city to cut Hood's last railroad and, as he put it, "make the matter certain." (ahc)

acknowledged to his wife, "we have made some dispositions to meet the exigency." "I suppose by tonight we shall know more of his designs," he added.

A key part of Hood's challenge in the last week of August was not merely guessing where beyond East Point the enemy would strike the Macon railroad, but how to guard it at all points. The Army of Tennessee on August 20, without cavalry, numbered just under 38,000 officers and men, who had to be stretched for a dozen and a half miles from the fortifications north of the city (Slocum's 8,700 troops hovered at the Chattahoochee rail bridge) down to Jonesboro—and those were crow-flight miles, not the actual course of the sinuous railroad. Hood's inability to both guard the city—on August 31 only French's division and Smith's militia were its defenders—and to stretch his army all along the M&W was his weakness, not any failure to have figured out his enemy's general goal. When Sherman wrote Schofield, "I don't think the enemy yet understand our movement," he was both unfairly belittling Hood and unwarrantedly complimenting himself on his own cleverness.

It is certainly worth pointing out that in none of his orders for a week, August 23-29, did Sherman specify where he wanted his troops to fall on the Macon railroad. On the 30th, when they got moving again, the six corps marched east on a broad, seven- or eight-mile front. They would get at the road at Jonesboro (Howard's three corps) or north of it (Schofield and Thomas). Sherman

"TO THE HONORED MEMORY OF THE SEVERAL HUNDRED UNKNOWN CONFEDERATE SOLDIERS REPOSING WITHIN THIS ENCLOSURE WHO FELL AT THE BATTLE OF JONESBORO AUGUST 31-SEPTEMBER 1." The Atlanta Ladies Memorial Association dedicated this memorial in the Cleburne Cemetery in 1934. Wilbur G. Kurtz added narrative text about the battle. (hp)

seems to have been content to set his troops in motion, then see what developed. Somewhere—it didn't really matter–Federal infantry would break the Rebels' lifeline.

"Atlanta is Ours and Fairly Won"

CHAPTER FOURTEEN

Hindsight is a wonderful thing for students of history, as we ask ourselves, why didn't John B. Hood send more troops to Jonesboro? At 1 p.m. on August 30, Shoup wired Hardee, "General Hood does not think the necessity will arise to send any more troops to Jonesborough today." Then, 20 minutes later, Shoup wrote Red Jackson, "General Hood does not think there can be a large force advancing upon Jonesborough." Of course, this latter statement was incorrect on the basis of what we know today: nearly 21,000 enemy infantry were marching on Jonesboro, a very "large force" indeed.

But we should also keep in mind that the other three Union corps, numbering some 35,000 troops, were *not* marching on Jonesboro.

As it turned out, these latter were the Federals who cut Hood's railroad to Macon. On the evening of August 30, Howard's infantry reached the Flint River—only a mile or so west of Jonesboro—crossed it, and approached the town, where they halted for the night. This development caused Hood to

In Atlanta's Oakland Cemetery is this monument to the several thousand unknown Confederate soldiers buried there. Known as the "Lion of Atlanta," it was commissioned in the early 1890s by memorial groups and dedicated on April 26, 1894—Confederate Memorial Day in the state. Sculpted of Georgia marble by T. M. Brady in Canton (north of Atlanta), the statue is based on the "Lion of Lucerne," the famed memorial to the Swiss Guards killed in 1792 trying to defend the royal family under attack in Paris during the French Revolution. (dd)

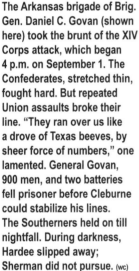

The Arkansas brigade of Brig. Gen. Daniel C. Govan (shown here) took the brunt of the XIV Corps attack, which began 4 p.m. on September 1. The Confederates, stretched thin, fought hard. But repeated Union assaults broke their line. "They ran over us like a drove of Texas beeves, by sheer force of numbers," one lamented. General Govan, 900 men, and two batteries fell prisoner before Cleburne could stabilize his lines. The Southerners held on till nightfall. During darkness, Hardee slipped away; Sherman did not pursue. (wc)

James M. Calhoun (1811-1875), wartime mayor of Atlanta.In the late 1830s, Calhoun, a lawyer in Decatur, was serving in the state House of Representatives when a bill came up about locating the terminus of a proposed railroad in a north Georgia town. Calhoun objected, remarking, "the terminus of that railroad will never be more than an eating house." (Was he wrong: "Terminus" became Atlanta.) (ahc)

Hood's last railway supply line, the M&W to Macon, was cut around 3 p.m. on August 31 when troops of Jacob Cox's division, XXIII Corps, struck the railroad eight miles north of Jonesboro. "The advance was sharply resisted by the enemy's cavalry," Cox reported, "but no infantry force was found." Several hours later, more Federals in the 3rd division, XIV Corps, led by Brig. Gen. Absalom Baird (shown here), also reached the railroad at Morrow, four miles north of Jonesboro. (loc)

call Generals Hardee, Lee, and Jackson to his headquarters for a consultation. The leaders decided to address the most immediate threat, so Hood ordered Hardee and Lee to march their troops to Jonesboro and "attack and drive the enemy at that place across the Flint River." By the time the Confederate forces reached the railroad town on August 31 (Hardee, sunrise; Lee, *ca.* 10 a.m.-1 p.m.) and deployed for their assault, it was 3 o'clock in the afternoon.

...the very time that elements of Jacob Cox's division of the XXIII Corps struck the Macon & Western at Quick Station, eight miles north of Jonesboro.

Cox saw no infantry before him, so his men easily drove off the hovering Rebel cavalry, then started tearing up the rail line. Southern horsemen to the north stopped two southbound trains; anticipating bad news, Hood was trying to get the army's reserve ordnance stores out of the city. The troopers told the engineers that Yankees were up ahead. Chugging back to the city in reverse, they arrived around 5 p.m.

The important news was immediately sent to Hood's headquarters. Tightening their grip on the M&W, around 6 p.m. troops of Absalom Baird's division of the XIV Corps reached the railroad at Morrow, four miles north of Jonesboro. Sherman's forces had finally succeeded in breaking Atlanta's last supply line.

These developments unfortunately made Hardee and Lee's attack at Jonesboro tactically pointless. Howard's army, dug in west of the town and anticipating the Rebel attack, easily repulsed it in two hours. The 1,700 casualties suffered by Confederates on the 31st are therefore tragically to be counted as lives wasted, as so often occurs in war. Adding to the tragedy, Federal losses were a 10th of that number.

Even before Hood learned of Hardee's/ Lee's repulse—the Yankees had cut the telegraph as well as the railroad—he knew that with Stewart's corps and the militia, he would have to evacuate the city. At 6 p.m., he sent orders by courier for Lee to march his troops back toward the city.

The army was now dangerously strung out and divided. Hood, Stewart, and Smith would

During the war Currier & Ives, headquartered in New York City, issued a number of speedily produced battle prints. Mark E. Neely and Harold Holzer, in *The Union Image* (2000), aptly point to their artistic crudeness, "evidence of the humble lack of sophistication of their patriotic purchasers." Caption for this "Battle of Jonesboro" hails Sherman's achievement in swinging his troops south of Atlanta, "the Rebel Genl. Hood being completely 'hoodwinked.'" (loc)

George Barnard included this image, "Destruction of Hood's Ordinance [sic] Train" in his Photographic Views of Sherman's Campaign (New York, 1866), a collection of some sixty photographs he had taken from Nashville to Charleston and Columbia. Barnard arrived in Atlanta in mid-September 1864, hired by Sherman's engineer Captain Poe to take pictures of the area. One of the first places he visited—along with the downtown railroad yards and McPherson's death-site—was that of the Rebels' blown-up ammunition train. Chimneys of the Atlanta Rolling Mill, also destroyed in the night of September 1-2, stand beside the tracks. (loc)

march south and rendezvous with Lee. Hardee was directed to hold on as best he could while the rest of the army marched to reunite with him.

On the morning of September 1, Confederates in Atlanta began to pack up what they could and planned to burn or blow up the rest. Food was given out to the populace and warehouses were opened on a first-come, first serve basis. In the afternoon, cannon too heavy to be rolled away were spiked. The troops started marching out around 5 o'clock.

The last to leave the city, cavalry and militiamen, set fire to the big buildings east of the city that had housed the rolling mill. Nearby, on the Georgia Railroad, they also put the torch to the two trains loaded with ammunition that had failed to escape. Twenty-eight cars packed with ordnance exploded, sending iron flying into the air and all around the vicinity. One hundred and fifty years later, archeologists

After the war, the vicinity of the Rolling Mill near the Georgia Railroad became site of the Fulton Bag and Cotton Mill, established in 1881. In the 1880s, a village was constructed for mill works called "Cabbagetown." The city has sprawled since then, but Atlantans still call the area Cabbagetown. (ahc)

digging in Oakland Cemetery's Potter's Field unearthed a lot of this metal.

"At 2 a.m. our brigade left Atlanta at a rapid gait," one Confederate remembered. "Just as we were leaving the suburbs the explosion of the magazines shook the city from center to circumference."

The explosions alerted Slocum at the Chattahoochee that something was up. He ordered early morning reconnaissance by his three divisions. The Federals saw the Rebel works abandoned, and farther on around 11 a.m., encountered Atlanta mayor James M. Calhoun, who formally surrendered the city.

Slocum sent word to Sherman, who had also heard the explosions at Jonesboro, 20 miles to the south. "About midnight there arose toward Atlanta sounds of shells exploding," he recalled in his memoirs. He could not be certain that the enemy were abandoning the city until he got the news from Slocum.

Meanwhile on the 1st, Howard's infantry attacked Hardee's. Though the Federals overran part of the Confederate lines—capturing Brig. Gen. Daniel Govan, 900 prisoners and eight field pieces—Hardee held on until nightfall, when he slipped away with his corps to find the rest of the army.

Sherman has been criticized for letting him do this, and in the next several days for allowing Hood to reassemble his army. A more aggressive Union general (think Ulysses S. Grant) would have chased and pounced on

On August 31, after ordering the evacuation of Atlanta, Hood's task was to unite the two widely separated halves of his army: Hardee and Lee at Jonesboro and Stewart's corps with the militia in the city. Hood directed Lee's infantry to march north on September 1 toward a junction with him. This left Hardee at Jonesboro to dig in and fend off any enemy attack on the 1st. "It now became necessary for me to act on the defensive," Hardee later wrote. (ahc)

Near the Warren house on the north edge of Jonesboro, this marker explains that after the withdrawal of Lee's corps, Hardee extended his line to the right, refusing it eastward across the railroad. Here, Jeff Davis's Federal XIV Corps attacked Confederates of Cleburne's division on September 1. (ahc)

A half-century ago, scholarship of the Atlanta campaign focused on the failure of Hardee's and S. D. Lee's attack, August 31, against Howard's Army of the Tennessee at Jonesboro. Here, a state historical marker placed in 1958 describes the action. Nowadays, we recognize it was the Federals' lodgment on the railroad eight miles north of Jonesboro, midafternoon of the 31st, which caused Hood to abandon Atlanta. Confederate headquarters knew this by 5 p.m. Yankees had cut the telegraph, so Hood would not learn of Hardee's repulse for hours after he had ordered the evacuation. (hmdd)

Hardee's contingent, then advanced to roll up the rest of the Rebel forces in detail. William T. Sherman, however, lacked the killer instinct and let Hood reunite his army in the next several days at Lovejoy's Station.

But Sherman had taken the prize city. "Atlanta is ours and fairly won," he telegraphed Halleck. A grateful Abraham Lincoln put out a call for 100-gun salutes to be fired at every arsenal and navy yard in the U. S.—including New Orleans and a few other Southern cities in Federal hands. He also issued a proclamation of thanks to General Sherman, his officers, and his men for having secured a great victory. "The marches, battles, sieges, and other military operations that have signalized this campaign must render it famous in the annals of war," he announced, "and have entitled those who have participated therein to the applause and thanks of the nation." The people of the *Confederate* nation, of course, felt much differently.

Despite the very different consequences of the campaign for each side, the total casualties were ironically similar. In his campaign report, Sherman posted these numbers for May-August 1864: 4,988 killed, 24,827 wounded, and 4,708 missing for a total of 34,523 officers and men lost. For their parts, Johnston and Hood for years after the war jousted with one another about the Atlanta campaign and failed to agree on casualty figures for the Army of Tennessee. A staff officer for General Hardee, Lt. W. L. Trask, apparently worked from army medical records and entered into his war diary that campaign casualties for the army totaled 3,044 killed, 18,962 wounded, and 12,983 missing, for a total of 34,979. This leads

"General Sherman's Victory—Rebel Prisoners Being Conducted to Atlanta from Jonesborough" read the caption for this woodcut illustration in *Harper's Weekly*, Oct. 1, 1864. At Jonesboro on September 1, Sherman achieved something he had not been able to do in the entire Atlanta campaign: in the words of the late Albert Castel, "a successful large-scale frontal assault." (hw)

historian Richard McMurry to assert that the Confederates incurred casualties of "about 35,000," a toll that "roughly equaled Union losses."

The Atlanta campaign, one may thus conclude, had been one of the costliest of the war.

After defeating Hardee at Jonesboro, Sherman allowed Hood to reassemble his army to the south while Slocum's XX Corps occupied Atlanta. Sherman himself did not arrive in the city until September 7. He brought his troops up from Jonesboro rather leisurely, instructing them to destroy more of the Macon & Western Railroad as they went. When all done, one Union officer estimated that they had wrecked 15 miles of the M&W, three-quarters of its 23-mile length from Jonesboro to Atlanta. (hw)

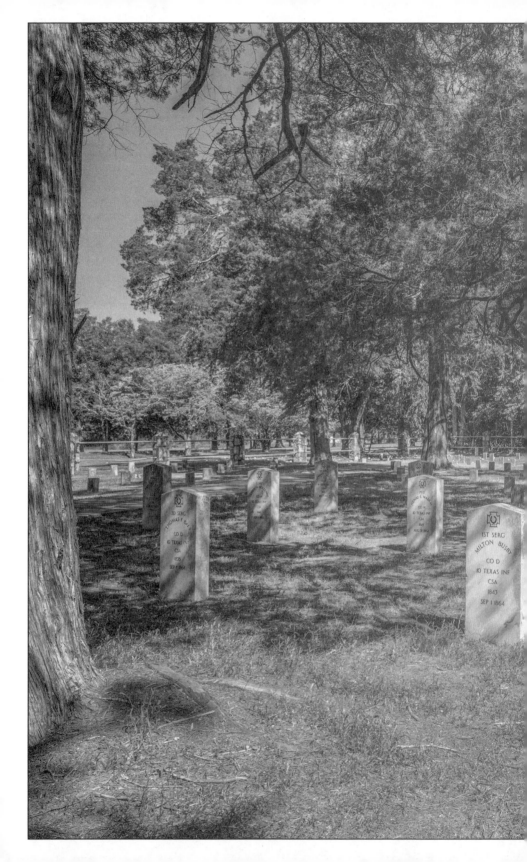

Measuring Sherman's Achievement

EPILOGUE

The news that Union forces had captured Atlanta thrilled the North. Newspapers quickly made the connection between Sherman's victory and Lincoln's vastly improved chances for re-election. "The political skies begin to brighten," announced the *New York Times*. "The dark days are over. We see our way out," the *Chicago Tribune* chimed in.

Sherman became an overnight hero across the North. "Genius," some papers exclaimed; his accomplishment was hailed as "brilliant" and "masterly."

Cump deserved the adulation. In the first half of the campaign, he had used his superior numbers in smart maneuvers, while on the front lines he kept his troops pounding away at the Rebels with shells and sorties. He had flanked Joe Johnston out of nine separate defensive positions from Dalton to the Chattahoochee. Alarmed Confederate leaders felt they had had no choice but to relieve Johnston, and put in his place a general known for his fighting qualities. "Atlanta had virtually been lost when Hood took command," Georgia Senator Ben Hill later admitted.

"We intend to make the cemetery a spot that will be an honor to the memory of our Confederate heroes." So declared an officer of the Atlanta Ladies Memorial Association of Cleburne Cemetery at Jonesboro in 1933. The next year, the ALMA dedicated its stone memorial inside the gated enclosure. Since that time, headstones have been neatly arrayed in the cemetery. A dramatic number denote soldiers in the 10th Texas Infantry—Granbury's Texas brigade held the left of Cleburne's division when the Federals attacked on September 1. (hp)

Reflecting later on the fall of Atlanta, Confederate President Davis told a friend, "I was not among those who deemed that result inevitable as soon as the enemy had crossed the Chattahoochee." He claimed that if Atlanta had to be given over to the enemy, he only wished that "manly blows had been struck for its preservation."

John Bell Hood had done at least that much, and more. Outnumbered and out-positioned by an enemy force just a few miles outside of the city, Hood had held onto it for a month and a half by a combination of attacking battles, spirited cavalry operations, and a mix of just plain determination and grit as he struggled to hold onto his last railroad supply line.

Sherman outmatched him in maneuvering. In late August, when Hood seemed to have stalemated his efforts to cut the railroad around East Point, Sherman had led fully six infantry corps, some 56,000 troops, in a wide-ranging sweep around East Point toward Rough and Ready/Jonesboro. Hood could not stretch his army that far, the Federals cut the railroad, and Hood had to evacuate the prize city.

What was the value of that prize? All of the factors that had made Atlanta such an important Confederate city at the start of 1864 had largely faded by the time the Yankees approached. Its valuable rolling mill and arsenal machinery had been moved away to other places. Atlanta had also been an important Southern supply center for the Army of Tennessee. In July 1863, the city's warehouses bulged with 1.8 million pounds of bacon; a year later no such stores of foodstuffs remained in the city. When the army hospitals were sent south, Atlanta also ceased to be an important Confederate medical center. With two of its railroads cut and a third—the Western & Atlantic— in enemy hands, the city also no longer functioned as a transportation hub.

Yet Atlanta remained an important symbol of Confederate defiance, and Northerners and Southerners alike knew its political significance during the U. S. presidential campaign. "If you want to know who is for McClellan," an editor in Albany, New York, advised, "mention Atlanta to them. The long face and the growl is sufficient." A soldier from North Carolina in Lee's army laconically admitted, "I am afraid that the fall of Atlanta will secure Lincoln's re-election."

* * *

Even before Sherman's forces launched their campaign to capture Atlanta, leaders on both sides realized its political ramifications. 1864 was a presidential election year in the United States. Abraham Lincoln's party would nominate him for re-election. The Democrats could be counted on to capitalize on Northerners' war weariness, to blame Lincoln for a failed war, and to call for a negotiated peace to end the death and suffering. There were indeed a large number of antiwar Northerners, nicknamed "Copperheads." If Union armies in the summer and fall of '64 did not win a major victory in the coming campaigns—if Robert Lee held Grant at bay before Richmond, and if Sherman failed before Atlanta—the Copperheads would argue that only a Democratic president could stop the war.

Southerners thus held out hope that the Northern peace party would win the election, and to help its chances, Atlanta had to be held. "Atlanta is, then, the great strategic point," predicted the Augusta (GA) *Constitutionalist* on May 1, 1864. "A crushing, decisive victory in Northwest Georgia will irretrievably crush the

President Lincoln, running for re-election in 1864, was so gloomy about his prospects that on August 23 he had his cabinet members sign a memorandum predicting defeat. By that time, the Rebel commerce raider *Alabama* had been sunk (June 19) and Farragut had won at Mobile Bay (August 5). But it was Sherman's capture of Atlanta on September 2 that markedly improved Lincoln's chances for a second term. (loc)

power of the enemy, and break down the war party of the North. A substantial victory now will lead to peace," the paper affirmed.

Two months into the campaign, there was still hope. Georgia Senator Benjamin H. Hill recorded then that if Sherman could be beaten and pressed back out of Georgia, "Lincoln's power will be broken, his re-election defeated . . . and we shall speedily end the war on our own terms."

Even a stalemate could help the Democrats' chances. As late as mid-July, with Lee holding his Petersburg lines and Hood holding his at Atlanta, a Democratic newspaper editor announced, "Lincoln is deader than dead." The president himself believed he would lose the election, predicting it in a memorandum that he did not show his Cabinet members, but which he made them sign on August 23. The next day, Gen. George McClellan, the party's presumptive nominee, told a supporter, "If I am elected, I will recommend an immediate armistice." With good reason then, a Richmond War Department clerk recorded in his diary on August 21, "Lincoln and his party are now environed with dangers rushing upon them from every direction. . . . [E]verything depends upon the result of the Presidential election in the United States."

But then Atlanta fell. Combined with Union admiral David Farragut's victory at Mobile in August, the news of Sherman's triumph turned the electoral tide in Lincoln's favor. "Sherman and Farragut have knocked the bottom out of the Chicago platform," exclaimed Secretary of War Edwin Stanton, referring to the Democrats' peace plank. Sheridan's thrashing of Jubal Early in the Shenandoah heartened Republicans even more. "Sheridan has knocked down gold and G. B. McClellan together," crowed one prominent Northerner. "The former is below 200, and the latter is nowhere."

For Confederates, the news from Atlanta was bad enough. "I am afraid that the fall of Atlanta will secure Lincoln's re-election," a Confederate soldier wrote home from Virginia on September 5. After hearing news of Early's defeats, Mary Boykin Chesnut, wife of Confederate Brig. Gen. James Chesnut, entered in her diary, "These stories of our defeats in the Valley fall like blows upon a dead body. Since Atlanta I have felt as if all were dead within me, forever."

Historians continue to share the understanding that Sherman's capture of Atlanta led to Lincoln's re-election and thus to the downfall of the Confederacy. Albert Castel posits the point in his definitive history of the Atlanta campaign, which he entitled, *Decision in the West* (1992)—the Confederates' last hope for independence rested with their holding onto Atlanta through the North's November election. Richard McMurry's *Atlanta 1864: Last Chance for the Confederacy* (2000) makes the same argument.

However long-standing, the Atlanta-Lincoln-Union victory hypothesis is not without critics or dissenters. William C. Davis is one, as he explains in his essay, "The Turning Point That Wasn't: The Confederates and the Election of 1864" (1996). Davis reminds us that back then, U.S. presidents were not inaugurated till early March, giving Lincoln and Union armies four months in which to launch offensive operations against the Confederacy's tottering forces and decisively defeat them before the new Democratic president took office. "Lee, his army, and Richmond as a result would inevitably have fallen before March 4,"

Maj. Gen. George B. McClellan accepted the Democratic Party's nomination for president in late August 1864, pledging no armistice with the Rebels without a return of the Southern states to the Union. But many (especially Confederates) believed that McClellan, if elected president, would seek an armistice to end the war without such conditions. It didn't matter. Lincoln won re-election handily on November 8, taking 212 electoral votes to McClellan's 21. The Democrat won only Delaware, Kentucky, and New Jersey. (loc)

he reasons. Moreover, McClellan was firmly on record that he favored a peace only if the Southern states returned to the Union— something that Jefferson Davis and his people were determined not to do. For these reasons, Davis concludes, "the notion of Lincoln's loss leading directly to Confederate independence is but a fable."

As we know, however, fables die hard. Civil Warriors will continue to debate the consequences of Atlanta's fall for some time to come. It may be too much to speculate that Lincoln would not have been re-elected on November 8 without Sherman's capture of Atlanta. There were other Union victories that summer and fall—Mobile Bay, Sheridan in the Valley of Virginia—but Atlanta was clearly the most important and dramatic of them all.

Conversely, we also cannot speculate that if Hood had somehow managed to hold Atlanta past November 8, and if Lincoln had lost, the Confederacy could have negotiated an armistice with President George McClellan and would have secured its independence.

History is what it is. The best we in today's armchair can conclude is that the North won the American Civil War, and that General William T. Sherman's capture of Atlanta was a signal event contributing to Union victory.

Cump Sherman was usually indifferent as to attire, but he dressed up for George Barnard to take his picture in Atlanta, late September 1864. He's in coat with epaulettes and even a sash around his waist. The general even took pride in how his horse looked. "I sent you a few days ago some photographs, of which Duke was very fine," he wrote his wife Ellen in October. (loc)

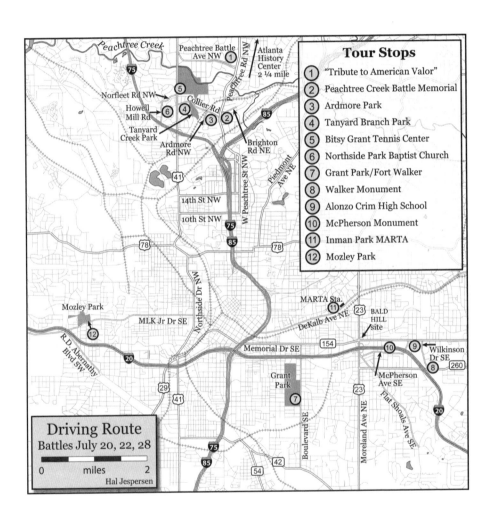

Tour Stops

1. "Tribute to American Valor"
2. Peachtree Creek Battle Memorial
3. Ardmore Park
4. Tanyard Branch Park
5. Bitsy Grant Tennis Center
6. Northside Park Baptist Church
7. Grant Park/Fort Walker
8. Walker Monument
9. Alonzo Crim High School
10. McPherson Monument
11. Inman Park MARTA
12. Mozley Park

Driving Route
Battles July 20, 22, 28

0 miles 2

Hal Jespersen

$\mathcal{D}$riving $\mathcal{T}$our

A TOUR OF THE
ATLANTA CAMPAIGN

Everyone knows that the city of Atlanta's growth since the war has sprawled over and obliterated its Civil War battlefields.

What not everyone knows is that today's Civil Warrior can actually put together an entertaining and informative itinerary to see the sites of the three big battles fought here in July 1864.

Let's remember, however, that at one time (long, long ago) these battlefields might actually have been preserved.

Confederate veterans living in Atlanta wanted the sites marked. In 1895, when the United Confederate Veterans held its annual reunion in the city, several vets prepared a map and tour-guide to more than seventy war-related sites, such as battery positions and headquarters locales.

A few years later some Atlanta businessmen conceived a "national military park" in the vicinity of the battle of Peachtree Creek north of downtown. The planners envisioned some 1,275 acres of then-residential property which could be bought for $300,000. Others proposed that land involved in the two battles in the eastern and western parts of the city also be purchased. They even described a twenty-five mile parkway to connect the three tracts.

Money, as always, killed the Atlanta park project, although it was kicked around for another three decades. In the late 1920s Wilbur G. Kurtz, Atlanta's indefatigable Civil War historian, could still see entrenchments in the city's suburbs. In the '30s, when the War Department evinced continued interest in a possible Atlanta military park, Kurtz showed

Atlanta's expansion since the war means that buffs seeking the three big battlefields of July 1864 have to experience the "urban landscape."

the officer around town. It was also Kurtz who in the 1950s wrote the texts of most of the state historical markers that dot the city and explain what happened here in 1864.

That's mostly what we'll see on a driving tour in the metro area.

Battle of Peachtree Creek, July 20

A good starting point is the Atlanta History Center (130 West Paces Ferry Road in Buckhead). Be sure to take in its permanent Civil War exhibit, "Turning Point"—one of the best in the country!

From the History Center, drive a few blocks to Peachtree Road, turn right, heading south. At about 1 ½ miles, before you come to the creek at the bottom of the slope, turn right onto Peachtree Battle Avenue and park near the traffic island with the stone memorial.

Peachtree Battle Avenue is a picturesque thoroughfare running just north of Peachtree Creek. But the Union line on July 20 ran almost a mile to the south, nearer to Collier Road. (dd)

Tour Stop 1

"Tribute to American Valor" was dedicated in 1935 to soldiers of both the Civil War and World War. Note the kepi and helmet, the musket and 1903 Springfield.

Walk across Peachtree (careful!). On the south side of the creek at Fairhaven Circle are a Georgia Civil War Heritage Trails plaque about the battle and a Sons of Confederate Veterans tablet honoring Confederate Brig. Gen. Clement H. Stevens, mortally wounded July 20. Also there is a Georgia Historical Commission/Kurtz (GHC) marker telling us that on July 19 Wood's and Newton's divisions, marching south from Buckhead, found that the Rebels had burned the bridge over the creek. Wood's men improvised one, engaged the Confederates on the other side, and drove them off. Newton crossed at dark. The next morning the

Federals marched south to the high ground on which Piedmont Hospital is situated ("Cardiac Hill," as we call it).

Return to your car and drive approximately ¾ of a mile south to Brighton Road on the left. Park beside the CVS.

TOUR STOP 2

A GHC marker, "Newton's Division," explains the deployment of Newton's three brigades. In the afternoon Walker's division struck the Federal line here and was shortly repulsed. Bate's division, to Walker's right, outflanked the left of Newton's line, but did not press hard against it.

Use extreme caution in hurrying across Peachtree. In front of the hospital is a white marble monument to "American Valor," dedicated on July 20, 1944, by the Atlanta Historical Society.

One of the most egregious instances of misplaced Civil War monuments in Atlanta is this small tablet, set in stone on Peachtree near Piedmont Hospital. It claims to mark the site on July 20 of Confederate Capt. E. P. Howell's battery during the battle of Peachtree Creek. The problem is that the marker, dedicated in 1919, is on the ridge occupied by Union troops that day. The battery was actually positioned a half-mile south.
(dd)

To the right on the sidewalk is a small granite marker for "Howell's Battery," placed here in 1919—problem is, it's in the wrong place. It claims that Confederate Capt. E. P. Howell's battery was here during the battle. NOT! How could it be, here in the middle of the Yankee line!? Howell himself had marked the site of his battery a half-mile to the south. More recently Kurtz and Atlanta historian Franklin Garrett called for the stone to be moved to its proper site, but no one has done anything.

Drive down Brighton and around Montclair to palisades. "Hardee's Attack" marker tells us that the battle started here around 3:30 or 4 p.m.

From Palisades turn right onto Peachtree, then left at the light onto Collier Road. After three blocks turn left onto Ardmore Drive.

TOUR STOP 3

At the bottom of the hill in Ardmore Park are three markers, stating that here Featherston's Mississippi brigade, advancing northward from the Confederates' outer entrenched line, struck

Wood's and Coburn's brigades of Ward's division, XX Corps. Notice the wording of "Featherston's Brigade": the Confederates dislodged Union skirmishers on the south side of Collier Road and "moved down the slope N. toward Coburn's and Wood's positions." "Down the slope"?! We're in low ground! In the '50s Kurtz not only wrote the markers' text but also advised on their placement. Up until a few years ago these markers were along Collier Road on both sides of the bridge over the Seaboard Coastline Railroad. But traffic accidents occurred on busy Collier when people stopped to read the markers, so these three were moved here to the park. But up until then they made more sense: Confederates charged across Collier Road and down the slope to its north where the Yankee infantry was posted. At least one marker has been moved back up the hill to Ardmore and Collier, describing the Mississippians' assault and repulse.

Return to Collier, turn left, drive downhill to Tanyard Branch Park.

TOUR STOP 4

Walk along Collier and across Tanyard Branch. "Scott's Brigade" marker tells us that Confederates marched here to strike the Federals north of Collier Road.

Cross Collier, turn right and walk up to the GHC maker, "Gap in Federal Line" in the front yard of 423 Collier Road. Col. Benjamin Harrison (yes, the future U. S. president) and his brigade had crossed Peachtree Creek the morning of July 20 and was posted in the low ground 350 yards north of here. The Federals were expecting no attack that afternoon, and a gap existed between the right of Ward's division and the left of Geary's. Kurtz: "The sudden dash of Scott's Alabama brigade across Collier Road briefly engulfed Harrison's right flank until reinforcements came, as Ward's division shifted toward the west, eliminating the gap with Geary. Scott's Confederates were driven south, back across the road."

Walk back down to Redland Road, east of the bridge over the branch. Andrew Jackson Collier had his grist mill 60 feet downstream (north) from this point. Decades after the war millstones and a wheel were found in the creek; the Atlanta Historical Society fixed them here in 1951.

Return to Tanyard Branch Park. A colorful Georgia Civil War Heritage Trails plaque describes the battle. Six metal tablets, set here in 1964, offer very wordy details on the campaign to this point and the battle of July 20. Text was written by Allen P. Julian, director of the Atlanta Historical Society.

Ned was a staunch defender of Joe Johnston—look for hints of bias in the markers. See the Confederate casualty figures Julian chose for the battle: 4,796 Southerners *hors de combat*. Sherman set forth this figure in his *Battles and Leaders* article of the 1880s, and Col. Julian accepted it!

Head out of the park, and turn left on Collier. At Walthall Drive is a marker for "Geary's Division." On July 20 Brig. Gen. John Geary's division was deployed on the ridge north of the road.

Incidentally, in the 1930s, when this neighborhood was being developed, Wilbur Kurtz was working for the City of Atlanta Planning Commission. He was thus able to get this street named for Confederate Maj. Gen. Edward C. Walthall.

Turn left on Walthall and drive to 1911 and the marker "33d N. J. State Flag." The regiment had been advanced to near here to hold high ground for a battery position. The Federals were overwhelmed by Scott's sudden attack. John Abernathy of the 27th Alabama is credited with capturing the regimental colors.

Turn around, across Collier; then turn right onto Overbrook Drive. It dead ends at Northside Drive; turn right. Enter Bitsy Grant Tennis Center; Bobby Jones Golf Course. Park in the lot to the left.

TOUR STOP 5

Four GHC markers are here, including "Williams' Division Deployed." Having crossed Peachtree Creek 750 yards to the north, Brig. Gen. Alpheus S. Williams's Federal division arrayed on this ridge. No attack was anticipated. Geary's division was a half mile east. A deep ravine separated the two. There was no road in 1864 where Northside Drive is now.

Next: the case of three more markers moved from their intended sites. Folks can more safely stop here to read them, but Kurtz's text was intended to fit topo references no longer valid at this site.

"Geary's Refused Line" was originally at

Suburban developers have constructed neighborhoods over much of the Peachtree Creek battlefield. But the ravine which runs north along Collier Road is so deep and wide it's not been built over. The wooded gully looks much like it did when O'Neal's Confederate brigade struggled through it on the afternoon of July 20. (dd)

Northside Drive and Collier Road, a half mile to the south. Geary's division had halted along this ridge when Brig. Gen. Edward O'Neal's brigade attacked. The Confederates forced Geary to bend the right of his line down the slope and beyond the deep ravine northward.

"O'Neal's Brigade" was also originally at Northside and Collier. O'Neal's troops struck the right of Geary's division and charged down the slope. Taking fire on both flanks from Geary and Williams, they had to fall back.

"O'Neal's Brigade at the Ravine" explains that O'Neal's Alabama and Mississippi troops temporarily broke the Federal line at this point.

From Bitsy Grant, turn left back onto Northside Drive, then a quick right onto Norfleet. As you drive, look to the left at the deep ravine into which O'Neal's Confederates charged. Turn left onto Howell Mill.

Look quickly to the right, in front of Chipotle to find "Maj. William C. Preston C.S.A." (hard to catch, as the GHC plaque parallels the road). Preston, an artillery battalion commander, was killed here while directing a battery of guns to support the attack of Brig. Gen. Daniel Reynolds's brigade. This was the last real action of the day. With Reynolds's repulse, around 6 p.m., the battle began to fizzle to sporadic skirmishing.

"Willie" was the brother of Sally Buchanan "Buck" Preston, to whom at the time General Hood was engaged to be married. Hood was deeply moved by Preston's death. Mary Chesnut records that months later Hood was seen sitting alone before a fire, visibly grieving over lost comrades. "He sees Willie Preston with his heart shot away," she wrote in her diary.

Continue heading south on Howell Mill. Just before I-75 pull in on the left to Northside Park Baptist Church.

Tour Stop 6

In the front yard is the grave of Confederate Sgt. William R. Moore, 1st Georgia Cavalry, who was killed north of Peachtree Creek July 17 as the Southerners contested the Yankees' advance. His body was brought to his churchyard and buried. Wheeler's Confederate Cavalry Association placed the present monument to him in 1900.

Battle of Bald Hill, July 22

The big battle fought east of the city on July 22 has come to be called the battle of Atlanta, but we purists bristle at such a misleading name when there were at least three sizable battles around Atlanta. Albert Castel and others have more accurately called it the battle of Bald Hill, and among some writers that name has stuck. I like the observation of Confederate Capt. Thomas Key, however: "As I know no name I call it the battle of the 22nd of July."

You can get on I-75 south at Howell Mill, drive about 5 miles through downtown to I-20 east (exit 247), then get off at the first exit (59A): Boulevard. Turn right onto Boulevard.

Within a half mile, you'll see Grant Park on the right. It was named for Lemuel P. Grant (1817-1893). During the war Grant was an engineer officer assigned to supervise the building of the fortifications surrounding the city. A prosperous landowner, in 1883 Grant donated more than 80 acres of this area for a city park. Another 44 were bought from Grant in 1890.

As you drive past the park, look for the last driveway into it. Turn right into the parking lot.

TOUR STOP 7

You'll see a Georgia Civil War Heritage Trails plaque, explaining Captain Grant's construction of the Atlanta defenses, including Fort "R."

…the earthen remains of which are right ahead of you. Grant's three dozen artillery forts originally had only alphabetic

A rarity in Atlanta: the earthen parapet of a Confederate artillery position. Here, Fort Walker in Grant Park. (dd)

designations. At some point "R" came to be called Fort Walker for the Confederate general killed in the battle of July 22. It is the only one left.

Wilbur Kurtz wrote the text for a metal plaque placed in 1938 by the Atlanta Ladies Memorial Association. It has now been attached to the granite base of a replica cannon placed here in the fall of 2014 by a local chapter of the United Daughters of the Confederacy. A GHCmarker explains that this fort was the southeast salient of the more than ten miles of Confederate rifle pits encircling the city.

"Glenwood Triangle" is a little plot of city-owned land at Glenwood Ave. and Wilkinson Rd., where the 1902 monument to Confederate General William H. T. Walker stands. (dd)

Drive back to I-20 and turn right onto the interstate. Take exit 61B onto Glenwood Avenue. Turn left, crossing over the highways.

To the right at the intersection of I-20 and Glenwood is the GHC marker, "Bate's Division at Terry Mill Pond." Bate's and Walker's divisions deployed here for the start of what they thought would be Hardee's flank attack.

Continue a short distance on Glenwood; turn left onto Wilkinson Drive.

TOUR STOP 8

Park beside the gas station next to the small tract with the upright cannon. Across Glenwood you can see the GHC marker, 'Terry's Mill Pond." On the morning of July 22 Tom Terry's grist mill pond, which had been impounded to form a small lake, disrupted the advance of Walker's division.

The upright cannon monument was dedicated July 22, 1902. This is the site where Maj. Gen. W. H. T. Walker was shot from his horse by a Federal picket just before his troops launched their assault. The GHC marker tells the story.

Drive north on Wilkinson and turn left on Memorial Drive. The second street on the right is Clay; the marker tells us "Battle of Atlanta Began Here." Brigadier General Elliott Rice's and Col. August Mersy's brigades had marched to this point by noon on the 22nd and "intercepted the surprise attack by Walker's & Bate's Divs." Across the street, a marker tells that the Federals repulsed Bate's attack.

Turn left at the next light, Clifton Street, and enter parking lot of Alonzo Crim High School.

TOUR STOP 9

At the corner is the GHC marker, "An Unexpected Clash." Both sides were surprised when Walker's/Bate's and Rice's/Mersy's troops clashed.

From the school, turn west (left) back onto Memorial. Turn left at the first light, onto Maynard; cross over I-20, and turn right onto McPherson.

TOUR STOP 10

At McPherson and Monument avenues is the monument to General McPherson. After the battle Federal soldiers marked the site of the general's death with a wooden sign nailed to a tree; Barnard photographed it during the occupation of September-November 1864. In 1877, U. S. army officers stationed in Atlanta resolved to raise a monument at the site and bought this small tract of land. The war department donated the cannon, which is set in a block of granite from Stone Mountain.

"An Unexpected Clash" is Wilbur Kurtz's marker text from the 1950s, when this site at Memorial Drive and Clifton Street was the J. C. Murphy High School. Now the school is named for Alonzo A. Crim, the first black superintendent of Atlanta schools. (dd)

Two GHC markers explain the fighting in this area and tell the story of McPherson's death.

Drive west on McPherson; pass Patterson and turn left on Haas. As you approach Glenwood, look to left for the GHC marker, "Cleburne Outflanked Left Wing, 17th A.C." Kurtz's text describes the attack by Cleburne's three brigades with struck the Federal flank and drove Giles Smith's division north to Leggett's Hill.

The site of Gen. McPherson's death, photographed by George Barnard in September 1864, is today in the middle of an east Atlanta neighborhood south of Interstate 20. (loc)

Turn right on Glenwood, right onto Flat Shoals and right again on Moreland Avenue, heading north. Cross I-20—there was once a marker here for Leggett's Hill; the hill itself was largely leveled during construction of the interstate here in the 1950s.

Continue north on Moreland; after driving under the railroad bridge, watch on the right for a sign to DeKalb Ave. Circle around and head west on DeKalb.

TOUR STOP 11

Park in the lot for the Inman Park/Reynoldstown MARTA station. Across Battery Place are four GHC markers: "The 15th Corps Sector," "Manigault's Brigade," "The Railroad Cut," and "The Pope House." Together they explain how about 4 p.m., Hood ordered Maj. Gen. Frank Cheatham's corps against this part of the Federal line, which ran north/

south. Brigadier General Arthur M. Manigault's South Carolina brigade overran the enemy line at the railroad cut before a Federal counterattack by Col. James S. Martin's and Brig. Gen. Joseph A. J. Lightburn's brigades drove it back.

Drive out of the MARTA parking, turn left back onto DeKalb Avenue. Turn left on DeGress Avenue. On the right, just before East Atlanta Baptist Church is the GHC marker, "Troup Hurt House." The two-story brick plantation house of George M. Troup

The East Atlanta Primitive Baptist Church was built in 1907 on what is now DeGress Avenue in the battlefield of July 22. In 1955 Wilbur Kurtz worked with church elders to get permission for his Troup Hurt house maker to be placed in the church's front yard. (dd)

Hurt stood here, a focus point of the Cyclorama mural.

Continue down DeGress. When it turns perpendicularly right, look to the left: "The DeGress Battery." During the battle Capt. Francis DeGress's four 20-pounder Parrotts were posted here. The Cyclorama shows Manigault's troops having overrun them as the Federals counterattack. The Yankees shot the battery horses to prevent the guns being withdrawn. The battery was retaken in Martin's and Lightburn's counterassault.

Battle of Ezra Church, July 28

Turn around; drive back to DeKalb Avenue and turn left. At Moreland, watch carefully for signs that will take you onto Moreland southbound. Drive south back to Interstate 20 and drive west through downtown to Exit 53, M. L. King Drive. At the end of the ramp, turn right onto MLK. Drive east; after a short distance, turn left to enter Mozley Park, 1565 Martin Luther King Drive (use the last park entrance on the left).

TOUR STOP 12

Park near the Georgia Civil War Heritage Trails plaque, which has recently been installed. A colorful map clearly depicts the attack of S. D. Lee's and Stewart's Corps on July 28.

Six metal tables and a separate map tablet are in place, compliments of the Georgia Historical Commission and the Georgia Civil War centennial Commission. Note their similarity to the tablets you've seen at Tanyard Branch Park. Like those, they explain rather verbosely the campaign events to this point and the battle of Ezra Church.

In the area are several GHC markers. One that is sorely missed once stood at the southeast corner of the park, "Site of Ezra Church." The wooden Methodist chapel, from which Federals removed

To construct Mozley Park off today's Martin Luther King Jr. Drive in east Atlanta, the city had to bulldoze over Civil War earthworks almost a century ago for the swimming pool and ball fields it built. (ahc)

benches for their barricades on July 28, did not survive the war. The marker post can be seen to the right of the six Julian plaques, alongside MLK Drive.

That's at times what happens to urban Civil War battlefields. Sometimes you visit them, and stuff has disappeared. You come again later, and some group might have placed a new marker.

Welcome to Atlanta, y'all!

Confederate Monuments in and around Atlanta

APPENDIX A
BY GOULD HAGLER

From the 1860s to the present day, Georgians have built numerous monuments to honor the Confederacy, its slain Confederate soldiers, their surviving comrades, and the stalwart women who supported the Cause.

Numerous monuments in the Atlanta area speak to us about the long and costly war in general and the Atlanta campaign more specifically. These memorials express the grief felt by mourning families and communities; they remind posterity of the bravery and determination of the Confederate soldiers, defeated but not dishonored; in stone and bronze they tell passersby what great events occurred on the very ground we tread on daily; they contain inscriptions stating the principles for which the Confederates fought; and they express relief that the suffering ended and that the riven nation reconciled.

The oldest of the Atlanta-area monuments dates to 1874. The most recent shown here is the Mother and Child statue in Marietta, built just four years ago. Others have been erected since then, an indication of the ongoing interest in the Civil War and the abiding respect still held for the men who served. It is noteworthy that Atlanta contains almost none of the classic soldier monuments common in other communities. However, regardless of the physical form the builders

"Mother and Child" was erected in 2012. For more information, see page 138. All photos in this section courtesy Gould Hagler. (gh)

chose for their memorials, we can learn from each of them about the events that occurred, about the people who participated in them, about their view—and their descendants' view—of their country's history and their role in it.

MOTHER AND CHILD

This moving work of art (as seen on pg. 136), placed in Marietta's Brown Park in 2012, is one of the newest of Georgia's Confederate monuments. We share the sadness of this war widow and her now fatherless child as they stand at the grave of their fallen soldier. In the nearby Marietta Confederate Cemetery lie the remains of thousands of men who left grieving families like this mother and her son.

MARIETTA OBELISK

This inscription on this 1908 obelisk in the Marietta Confederate Cemetery quotes from Father Ryan's "The Sword of Lee."

> *They sleep the sleep of our noble slain,*
> *Defeated, yet without a stain,*
> *Proudly and peacefully.*

OAKLAND OBELISK

This obelisk stands among the thousands of Confederate graves in Atlanta's Oakland Cemetery. The Atlanta Ladies Memorial Association dedicated this monument in 1874. A brief inscription says all that needs saying: *Our Confederate Dead.*

OAKLAND LION

Near the obelisk the brave Lion of Atlanta in his permanent sleep represents the unknown and uncounted war dead who are buried nearby. The Atlanta Ladies Memorial Association dedicated this famous sculpture in 1895.

JONESBORO

The graves in Jonesboro's Patrick R. Cleburne Cemetery are laid out in the pattern of the St. Andrew's Cross. A memorial arch welcomes the visitor to the burial ground; on a stone in the center an inscription penned by Wilbur Kurtz tells the story of the battle of Jonesboro.

LOVEJOY

In the dark hour of defeat, just days after the fall of Atlanta, members of the Sigma Chi fraternity assembled in Lovejoy and resolved to carry on as brothers, come what may. In 1939 the fraternity commemorated this initial meeting of its Constantine Chapter with this massive Sigma Chi cross.

PALMETTO

In late September the Army of Tennessee camped in Palmetto, where Jefferson Davis consulted with Hood and addressed the troops. On September 29 the aggressive general advanced to attack Sherman's supply line. The United Daughters of the Confederates (UDC) built this monument in 1906.

ROSWELL

In 2000 the Sons of Confederate Veterans erected this fluted column in Roswell in honor of the mill workers, mostly women, who in 1864 were taken as prisoners. With their children they were taken by wagon to Marietta and transported north by train. Some of these displaced persons made it home; most did not.

DECATUR

The monument at the old DeKalb County Courthouse dates to 1908. It contains several long inscriptions, including this emphatic apologia:

THESE MEN HELD THAT THE
STATES MADE THE UNION,
THAT THE CONSTITUTION IS THE
EVIDENCE OF THE COVENANT,
THAT THE PEOPLE OF THE STATE
ARE SUBJECT TO NO POWER
EXCEPT AS THEY HAVE AGREED,
THAT FREE CONVENTION BINDS
THE PARTIES TO IT, THAT THERE
IS SANCTITY IN OATHS AND
OBLIGATION IN CONTRACTS,
AND IN DEFENSE OF THESE
PRINCIPLES
THEY MUTUALLY PLEDGED THEIR
LIVES,
THEIR FORTUNES AND THEIR
SACRED HONOR.

WESTVIEW

Atlanta's historic Westview Cemetery contains this beautiful monument, unusual in that it was commissioned by the soldiers themselves. The Confederate Veterans' Association of Fulton County dedicated this statue in 1889 in memory of their dead comrades. A carving on the base shows in the midst of battlefield debris a hastily-dug

grave, the kind in which many of their fallen brothers were buried. One of the inscriptions tells how the survivors cherished the peace they lived to enjoy: "They shall beat their swords into ploughshares, and their spears into pruning hooks: nation shall not lift sword against nation, neither shall they learn war any more."

PEACHTREE CREEK (PIEDMONT HOSPITAL)

Eighty years after the Civil War, the descendants of men who fought against each other united to fight together against the Axis Powers. In 1944, in a tribute to American valor, the Atlanta Historical Society placed this memorial stone on Peachtree Road in honor of all the men who clashed at the battle of Peachtree Creek. An inscription provides an account of the Confederate attack on Sherman's forces on July 20.

PIEDMONT PARK PEACE MONUMENT

This magnificent sculpture at the 14th Street entrance to Piedmont Park was built by the Old Guard of the Gate City Guard in 1911. The weary soldier gazes up at the angel, who declares "Cease firing, peace is proclaimed."

RHODES HALL

Stone is the most common medium used for Confederate monuments. Many others are made of bronze. This unique memorial is made of stained glass. Amos Rhodes commissioned this masterpiece for his mansion on Peachtree Street, now the headquarters for the Georgia Trust for Historic Preservation. The nine stained-glass windows in three panels depict four scenes from the history of the Confederacy: the inauguration of President Davis, the bombardment of Fort Sumter, the battle of Manassas, and the surrender of Lee at Appomattox.

A small window, hidden in a closet beneath the stairs, shows the Confederate Battle Flag and other symbols of the fallen nation. The cryptic location of this window represents the sentiment expressed in the new century that the Cause should be remembered but the time had come to move on. Amos Rhodes was saying that it was time to put the flag away.

GORDON STATUE

John B. Gordon rose to the rank of major general in the Army of Northern Virginia, a remarkable achievement for a 32-year-old man with no formal military training. This statue at the State Capitol portrays a more mature Gordon as the first commander in chief of the United Confederate Veterans. He served one term as governor and represented Georgia in two terms in the United States Senate.

The statue is the work of the sculptor Solon Borglum, whose brother Gutzon began the Stone Mountain carving.

FATHER O'REILLY

This memorial stone at Atlanta's City Hall honors Father Thomas Patrick O'Reilly, pastor of the Church of the Immaculate Conception, credited with saving his church and four others from destruction as Sherman prepared to leave Atlanta for the sea.

This monument was built in 1945 by the five congregations whose buildings were saved, the Atlanta Historical Society and the City of Atlanta.

STONE MOUNTAIN

The mammoth high-relief carving on Stone Mountain is the grandest and most famous memorial to the Confederacy. The carving was begun by Gutzon Borglum in 1923. After delays brought on by financial problems, artistic disputes, depression and war, the State of Georgia took on the project in 1958 and completed the monument with its revised design: Lee, Davis, and Jackson on horseback. The monument was dedicated in 1970.

The mountain and the park surrounding it are owned by the State of Georgia, which created the Stone Mountain Memorial Association to oversee the development and preservation of Stone Mountain as a Confederate Memorial and public recreation area.

GOULD HAGLER *is a reitred lobbyist for the insurance industry. He is the author of* Georgia's Confederate Monuments: In Honor of a Fallen Nation *(Mercer University Press, 2014).*

Civil War Collections at The Atlanta History Center

APPENDIX B
BY GORDON JONES

The Atlanta History Center is the premier Civil War museum, research center, and interpretive site in the Southeastern United States.

Founded in 1926 as the Atlanta Historical Society, the private non-profit Atlanta History Center is located in Midtown Atlanta on a beautiful 33-acre campus. Here, the 150,000 square-foot Atlanta History Museum houses one of the nation's finest and most comprehensive Civil War artifact collections, including more than 11,000 objects from the collections of Beverly DuBose, Thomas S. Dickey, and George W. Wray, Jr. Because it represents at least one of almost every type of firearm, edged weapon, uniform, and accoutrement used during the Civil War, the Center's Civil War collection is considered among the finest and most comprehensive Civil War collections in the world. In size and scope, it is comparable only to the National Park Service Collection.

The Kenan Research Center houses a 42,000 square-foot library with more than 15,000 cubic feet of records, including 33,000 published volumes, more than 2,000 manuscript and photograph collections, and 7,800 rolls of microfilm. Included is an extensive collection of Civil War materials such as the Wilbur G. Kurtz collection of maps, research notes, and illustrations; a set of William T. Sherman's original orders written during the Atlanta Campaign; the diary of Samuel P. Richards, a British bookseller living in Atlanta during the siege

The Atlanta History Center's permanent Civil War exhibit, "Turning Point," showcases 1,400 items in ten rooms, each of which offers a theme. At the start, one is asked the key questions of the war, such as "Should all Americans adopt the North's vision of industry and wage labor?" and "Could America's future include the Southern vision of agriculture with slave labor?"
(ahc)

of the city; and numerous letters and diaries written by Union and Confederate soldiers. The library also includes military manuals, regimental histories, genealogical guides, and technical reference works for collectors.

Among three historic houses located on the campus is the Smith family farm, a typical north Georgia farmstead of the 1860s. Visitors exploring the farm encounter living history interpreters portraying the various family, friends, and workers of the household and are invited to participate in conversations and assist with activities. The Atlanta History Center also owns and operates the Margaret Mitchell House and Museum on Peachtree Street. In 2017, the Center will become home to the 1886 cyclorama painting, *The Battle of Atlanta*, formerly housed in Atlanta's Grant Park.

Many of the Center's most significant Civil War artifacts and documents are displayed

One area of "Turning Point" examines the several branches of military service. In "A Soldier's Job: Infantry," a preserved tree limb riddled with minie balls demonstrates the deadly effect of massed rifle fire on the battlefield. Navy frock coats from each side are displayed in "A Sailor's Job: The Navies." (ahc)

in the 9,200-square-foot exhibition *Turning Point: The American Civil War,* which is located along the main hallway of the Atlanta History Museum. One of five signature exhibitions in the museum (including those for golfing great Bobby Jones and the Olympic Games), *Turning Point* tells the story of the war from its earliest origins through Reconstruction and beyond. The title has two meanings: the Civil War as the seismic turning point in American history, and the Atlanta fampaign of 1864 as one of three major turning points within the war itself. Here visitors will find more than 1,500 Union and Confederate artifacts, including cannons, uniforms, firearms, flags, and soldiers' personal gear. Within the exhibition's ten rooms, photos, maps, text panels and videos provide the context, explaining how and why the war was fought. An audio tour, narrated by curator Gordon Jones and collector Beverly DuBose, III, is available at the admissions desk.

Highlights of the exhibition include a sword presented to Gen. Howell Cobb by the Provisional Congress of the Confederate States in 1861; Gen. John B. Gordon's dress uniform; a handwritten copy of Gen. Lee's General Order Number Nine; the flag of the U.S.S. *Hartford* from the battle of Mobile Bay; and the logbooks of the C.S.S. *Shenandoah.*

Other artifacts are more mundane but equally as powerful in telling personal stories of soldiers at war: a U. S. Army hospital flag and medicine chest; an original piece of Army bread or "hardtack"; a rifled shell for the Confederate cannon "Whistling Dick" made famous at the siege of Vicksburg; a calfskin knapsack; a brass drum; a Medal of Honor and other artifacts of the U. S. Colored Troops; English arms and equipment imported through the blockade into the Confederacy; and a U. S. 3-inch ordnance rifle with its limber, both on original wooden carriages.

Side-by-side comparisons of Union and Confederate firearms, swords, and accoutrements demonstrate the northern industrial capacity that eventually overwhelmed the slave-based pre-industrial Southern economy. Nearby, ritual mourning artifacts and a wooden grave marker testify to the strain of the war on the home fronts of both sides.

Some of the most intriguing artifacts pertain to the Atlanta campaign of 1864: the Confederate flag that flew over Atlanta at the time of its surrender; a U. S. six-mule army supply wagon used by the XX Corps during the Atlanta campaign; and Gen. Patrick Cleburne's presentation sword. The case entitled "Five Ordinary Men: Two Extraordinary Days" highlights the personal effects of men who fought at the battles of Peachtree Creek and Atlanta, including two bullet-torn uniforms, the sword worn by Gen. William H. T. Walker when he was killed on July 22, and the sword and revolver used by Union Capt. Francis DeGress during the same battle. Nearby is the diary kept by ten-year-old Carrie Berry during the siege of Atlanta and a letter written by a distraught Atlanta wife beseeching her husband in the Confederate Army to come home.

A final section of the exhibition, "The Search for Meaning," explores how the Civil War continues to impact us today. The war took at least 670,000 American lives—including an estimated 50,000 civilians—but freed four million enslaved people and confirmed the authority of the national government. A wall panel here challenges visitors with the question, "What does the Civil War mean to us today?"

"Turning Point" concludes with a section, "The Search for Meaning 1880—1945," with the regalia worn by aging veterans of the Grand Army of the Republic and the United Confederate Veterans. The words of one ex-Federal in 1882 are displayed: "I would rather have my boy stand by my grave and say, 'My father was wounded at the Wilderness, and fought with Sheridan at Five Forks, and saw Lee surrender at Appomattox' than to have him say that I was a millionaire, or a member of the United States Senate." (ahc)

Turning Point: The American Civil War goes a long way toward answering that question.

The Atlanta History Center is located at 130 West Paces Ferry Road, Atlanta, Georgia, and is open from 10 a.m. to 5:30 p.m. Mondays through Saturdays and noon to 5:30 p.m. on Sundays. The Kenan Research Center operates during the same hours Wednesdays through Saturdays. For more information call 404-814-4000 or see the website at www. atlantahistorycenter.com.

DR. GORDON L. JONES *is Senior Military Historian and Curator at the Atlanta History Center, where he has worked since 1991.*

The Battle of Atlanta on Canvas: A Brief History of the Atlanta Cyclorama

APPENDIX C
BY GORDON JONES

In the 1880s, before the advent of motion pictures, massive fifty-foot high, 360-degree cyclorama paintings were the virtual reality time machines of their day. Hung in a circle to be viewed from the inside, these paintings gave audiences a chance to "see" and "feel" historical events from the Crucifixion to the Franco-Prussian War. In the United States, the cyclorama fad produced at least twenty circular paintings of seven different Civil War battles: Shiloh, Second Manassas, Gettysburg, Vicksburg, Chattanooga, Atlanta, and the battle between the *Monitor* and the *Merrimac* (*Virginia*).

As popular entertainment, cycloramas soon gave way to movies and, by the early 1900s, nearly all were lost to fire, bankruptcy, or neglect. Today, only two Civil War cycloramas survive on exhibit: *The Battle of Gettysburg* and *The Battle of Atlanta*.

The Battle of Atlanta was created in Milwaukee by the American Panorama Company. In 1883, company manager William Wehner hired a team of artists from Germany and Austria, many of whom already had experience painting cycloramas in Europe. After initial success with *The Battle of Chattanooga and Storming of Missionary Ridge*, the artists came to Atlanta in the fall of 1885 to study the battlefield, which remained largely as it had been in 1864. The artists erected

Northerners shoot the horses of Capt. Francis DeGress's Illinois battery to prevent the Rebels from hauling away its four 20-pounder Parrotts. The Union counterattack succeeded in recapturing the cannon. (ahc)

General Logan gallops ahead, rallying his troops. Observers wonder why, in hot July temperatures, he is dressed in full dress wool frock coat and high boots. Students of the Cyclorama are still pouring over the extent to which the postwar artists may have embellished their painted depiction of events of the battle of July 22, 1864. (ahc)

a 40-foot-tall tower near the corner of present-day Moreland and DeKalb Avenues from which they sketched the landscape and noted troop positions. The artists favored this vantage point not only because of its dramatic potential, but also because a rival cyclorama company had already completed sketches for another depiction of the battle from the perspective of Bald Hill (the rival project was never completed).

Back in its Milwaukee studio, the American Panorama Company produced two identical copies of *The Battle of Atlanta* in 1886. The first—the one that survives today—was exhibited in Minneapolis, Indianapolis, and Chattanooga before coming to Atlanta in 1892. The second was exhibited in Detroit and Baltimore until 1899; no trace of it survives today.

The Battle of Atlanta depicts the action of July 22, 1864, at approximately 4:45 p.m. Here, elements of the Union XV and XVI Corps led by Maj. Gen. John A. "Black Jack" Logan, are shown counterattacking Cheatham's corps, which had earlier succeeding in breaking the Union line and capturing the twenty-pounder Parrott rifles of DeGress's battery. The painting thus highlights the battle's most pivotal and dramatic moment, a point not lost on Northern audiences watching the charismatic Logan riding to the rescue followed closely by Francis DeGress, intent on regaining his lost guns.

Despite folklore to the contrary, there is no evidence that Logan sponsored the $40,000 painting nor that it had anything to do with his 1884 vice presidential bid. Instead, the prominent placement of Logan is due mainly to Theodore Davis, a wartime illustrator for

Harper's Weekly who had accompanied Sherman's staff and was a personal friend of Logan and DeGress. As historical advisor to the American Panorama Company, Davis insisted that cycloramas would draw bigger audiences if they included famous personalities. In September 1886, three months before his death, Logan viewed the painting in its Minneapolis building, supposedly remarking, "ATLANTA is unquestionably the best war panorama which has been painted." A memorial service was held for him there in January 1887.

In February 1892, *The Battle of Atlanta* received an enthusiastic reception in the city that bore its name. Mindful of the sympathies of his new Southern audience, promoter Paul Atkinson advertised the scene of Cheatham's breakthrough as "The only Confederate victory ever painted." Nevertheless, Atlanta audiences soon tired of their new attraction, and Atkinson was forced to declare bankruptcy. In 1893, Atlanta businessman and philanthropist George V. Gress bought the painting at a fire-sale price and moved it to Lemuel P. Grant Park, where visitors could also see remains of Atlanta's defensive fortifications. In 1898, Gress donated the painting to the City of Atlanta.

Following years of public outcry, the dilapidated wooden building in Grant Park was replaced at city expense in 1921 with a new "fireproof" steel and brick building that would also house other Confederate "relics," including the locomotive *Texas*, hero of "The Great Locomotive Chase." Fifteen years later, a team of

After Confederates of Brig. Gen. Arthur Manigault's South Carolina brigade had broken through the Union XV line, Maj. Gen. "Black Jack" Logan organized a coun05charge. This segment of the Cyclorama shows Federals in the foreground advancing against Rebels beside and behind the two-story red brick house of George M. Troup Hurt. The Georgia Railroad cuts through toward the west, with Atlanta's skyline in the distance. (ahc)

One of the enduring legends of the Cyclorama is that two brothers—one fighting for the South, one for the North—met in the battle of Atlanta, one caring for the other. When the painting was exhibited in Chattanooga, the two were dubbed the Martin Brothers of Tennessee; when the painting came to Atlanta a year later, the figures became the Carter Brothers of Georgia. Though the story is fictitious, it represents the artist's attempt to portray wartime camaraderie and post-war reconciliation between the two sides. (ahc)

local artists, including future *Gone With the Wind* historical advisor Wilbur Kurtz, added 128 plaster figures to the foreground diorama as well as a few more Confederate soldiers to the painting itself where the composition was thought to be artistically (and politically) unbalanced.

By the 1970s, what had become known simply as the Atlanta Cyclorama was experiencing its worst crisis ever: absent maintenance for nearly forty years, it was rapidly deteriorating. At the same time, a tectonic shift in city politics resulted in the election of Maynard Jackson, the city's first African-American mayor. Fearing that Jackson would not care for "their" Cyclorama, some white Atlantans proposed that it be moved to the Confederate memorial park at Stone Mountain. Others suggested a new downtown location. Mayor Maynard Jackson responded: "It's one battle where the right side won. I'm going to make sure that depiction of that battle is saved." Jackson made good on his promise: between 1979 and 1982, at a cost of some $9 million, the painting was repaired and reinforced while still in its 1921 building.

Although Mayor Jackson's initiative saved the Atlanta Cyclorama from immediate destruction, fundamental problems remained. In a building too small for the painting's circumference (a six-foot-wide strip had to be removed from the painting in 1921), the canvas suffered from improper tensioning and excessive moisture, not to mention sharply declining public visitation. In 2012, a task force headed by Atlanta Mayor Kasim Reed determined that the best way to save the Cyclorama would be to move it into a larger and safer building at a venue offering long-term financial stability.

The Atlanta History Center, a private non-profit museum and research center on a thirty-three-acre campus, was able to offer the necessary physical and staff infrastructure—as well as private funding. In 2013, a gift of $10 million from Lloyd and Mary Ann Whitaker provided not only an endowment for a new cyclorama building at the Center but also served to jump-start a $32 million capital campaign for re-housing and restoring this national treasure.

On July 23, 2014, 150 years after the Battle of Atlanta, the Atlanta History Center signed a 75-year lease agreement with the City of Atlanta for the cyclorama painting and its associated artifacts (including the *Texas*). In late 2016, *The Battle of Atlanta* was moved to the Center, where visitors will be able to see the progress of restoration before its grand opening, complete with four new exhibit galleries, in 2018.

Federals of Col. August Mersy's brigade charge to restore the Union line and retake a battery of Parrott guns which the Rebels have captured by the Hurt house. Kennesaw Mountain is in the far distance. (ahc)

DR. GORDON L. JONES *is Senior Military Historian and Curator at the Atlanta History Center, where he has worked since 1991.*

ATLANTA CAMPAIGN,
JULY 18-SEPTEMBER 2, 1864

MILITARY DIVISION OF THE MISSISSIPPI
Maj. Gen. William T. Sherman

Chief of Artillery: Brig. Gen. William F. Barry
Medical Director: Lt. Col. Edward D. Kittoe
Chief of Ordnance: Capt. Thomas G. Baylor
Chief Engineer: Capt. Orlando M. Poe
Headquarters Guard: *7th Company, Ohio Sharpshooters*

ARMY OF THE CUMBERLAND
Maj. Gen. George H. Thomas

Chief of Artillery: Brig. Gen. John M. Brannan
Medical Director: Surg. George E. Cooper
Chief Engineer: Lt. Henry C. Wharton
Chief of Ordnance: Lt. Otho F. Michaelis
Escort: *Co. I, 1st Ohio Cavalry*

FOURTH CORPS Maj. Gen. Oliver O. Howard
Chief of Artillery: Capt. Lyman Bridges
FIRST DIVISION: Maj. Gen. David S. Stanley
First Brigade: Maj. Gen. Charles Cruft; Col. Isaac M. Kirby
21st Illinois • 38th Illinois • 31st Indiana • 81st Indiana • 1st Kentucky
2nd Kentucky • 90th Ohio • 101st Ohio

Second Brigade: Brig. Gen. Walter C. Whitaker; Col. Jacob E. Taylor
*96th Illinois • 115th Illinois • 35th Indiana • 21st Kentucky • 40th Ohio
51st Ohio*

Third Brigade: Col. William Grose; Col. P. Sidney Post
*59th Illinois • 75th Indiana • 80th Illinois • 84th Illinois • 9th Indiana
30th Indiana • 36th Indiana • 84th Indiana • 77th Pennsylvania*

Divisional Artillery: *Indiana Light, 5th Battery • Pennsylvania Light,
Battery B*

SECOND DIVISION: Brig. Gen. John Newton
First Brigade: Col. Francis T. Sherman; Brig. Gen. Nathan Kimball
*36th Illinois • 44th Illinois • 73rd Illinois • 74th Illinois • 88th Illinois
15th Missouri • 24th Wisconsin • 28th Kentucky*

Second Brigade: Brig. Gen. George D. Wagner; Col. John W. Blake
*100th Illinois • 40th Indiana • 57th Indiana • 26th Ohio • 97th Ohio
28th Kentucky*

Third Brigade: Brig. Gen. Charles G. Harker; Brig. Gen. Luther P.
Bradley
*22nd Illinois • 27th Illinois • 42nd Illinois • 51st Illinois • 79th Illinois
3rd Kentucky • 64th Ohio • 65th Ohio • 125th Ohio*

Divisional Artillery: *1st Illinois Light, Battery M • 1st Ohio Light,
Battery A*

Third Division: Brig. Gen. Thomas J. Wood
First Brigade: Brig. Gen. August Willich; Col. William H. Gibson;
Col. Richard H. Nodine
*25th Illinois • 35th Illinois • 89th Illinois • 32nd Indiana • 8th Kansas
15th Ohio • 49th Ohio • 15th Wisconsin*

Second Brigade: Brig. Gen. William B. Hazen
*59th Illinois • 6th Indiana • 5th Kentucky • 6th Kentucky • 23rd Kentucky
1st Ohio • 6th Ohio • 41st Ohio • 71st Ohio • 93rd Ohio • 124th Ohio*

Third Brigade: Brig. Gen. Samuel Beatty; Col. Frederick Knefler
79th Indiana • 86th Indiana • 9th Kentucky • 17th Kentucky • 13th Ohio
19th Ohio • 59th Ohio

Divisional Artillery: *Illinois Light, Bridges's Battery • Ohio Light, 6th Battery*

FOURTEENTH CORPS Maj. Gen. John M. Palmer
FIRST DIVISION: Brig. Gen. Richard W. Johnson;
Brig. Gen. John H. King

First Brigade: Brig. Gen William P. Carlin; Col. Anson G. McCook
104th Illinois • 42nd Indiana • 88th Indiana • 15th Kentucky • 2nd Ohio
33rd Ohio • 94th Ohio • 10th Wisconsin • 21st Wisconsin

Second Brigade: Brig. Gen. John H. King; Col. William Stoughton;
Col. Marshall F. Moore
*11th Michigan • 15th U. S. (6 companies Second Battalion) • 15th U. S.
(9 companies First and Second Battalions) • 16th U. S. (4 companies First
Battalion) • 16th U. S. (4 companies Second Battalion) • 18th U. S. (8
companies First and Third Battalions) • 18th U. S. (Second Battalion)
19th U. S. (First Battalion and A, Second Battalion)*

Third Brigade: Col. Benjamin Scribner; Col. Josiah Given;
Col. Marshall F. Moore
*37th Indiana • 38th Indiana • 21st Ohio • 74th Ohio • 78th Pennsylvania
79th Pennsylvania • 1st Wisconsin*

Divisional Artillery: *1st Illinois Light, Battery C • 1st Ohio Light, Battery I*

SECOND DIVISION: Brig. Gen. Jefferson C. Davis
First Brigade: Brig. Gen. James D. Morgan
*10th Illinois • 16th Illinois • 60th Illinois • 10th Michigan
14th Michigan • 17th New York*

Second Brigade: Col. John G. Mitchell
*34th Illinois • 78th Illinois • 98th Ohio • 108th Ohio • 113th Ohio
121st Ohio*

Third Brigade: Col. Daniel McCook; Col. Oscar F. Harmon; Col. Caleb J. Dilworth
85th Illinois • 86th Illinois • 110th Illinois • 125th Illinois • 22nd Indiana 52nd Ohio

Divisional Artillery: *2nd Illinois Light, Battery I • Wisconsin Light, 5th Battery*

THIRD DIVISION: Brig. Gen. Absalom Baird
First Brigade: Brig. Gen. John B. Turchin; Col. Moses B. Walker
19th Illinois • 24th Illinois • 82nd Indiana • 23rd Missouri 11th Ohio 17th Ohio 31st Ohio • 89th Ohio • 92nd Ohio

Second Brigade: Col. Ferdinand Van Derveer; Col. Newell Gleason
75th Indiana • 87th Indiana • 101st Indiana • 2nd Minnesota • 9th Ohio 35th Ohio • 105th Ohio

Third Brigade: Col. George P. Este
10th Indiana • 74th Indiana • 10th Kentucky • 18th Kentucky • 14th Ohio 38th Ohio

Divisional Artillery: *Indiana Light, 7th Battery; Indiana Light, 19th Battery*

TWENTIETH CORPS: Maj. Gen. Joseph Hooker
FIRST DIVISION: Brig. Gen. Alpheus S. Williams
First Brigade: Brig. Gen. Joseph F. Knipe
5th Connecticut • 3rd Maryland Detachment • 123rd New York • 141st New York 46th Pennsylvania

Second Brigade: Brig. Gen. Thomas H. Ruger
27th Indiana • 2nd Massachusetts • 13th New Jersey • 107th New York 150th New York • 3rd Wisconsin

Third Brigade: Col. James S. Robinson
82nd Illinois • 101st Illinois • 45th New York • 143rd New York • 61st Ohio 82nd Ohio

Divisional Artillery: *1st New York Light, Battery I • 1st New York Light, Battery M*

SECOND DIVISION: Brig. Gen. John W. Geary
First Brigade: Col. Charles Candy
5th Ohio • 7th Ohio • 29th Ohio • 66th Ohio • 28th Pennsylvania
147th Pennsylvania

Second Brigade: Col. Adolphus Buschbeck; Col. John T. Lockman;
Col. Patrick H. Jones
33rd New Jersey • 119th New York • 134th New York • 154th New York
27th Pennsylvania • 73rd Pennsylvania • 109th Pennsylvania

Third Brigade: Col. David Ireland; Col. George A. Cobham
60th New York • 78th New York • 102nd New York • 137th New York
149th New York • 29th Pennsylvania • 111th Pennsylvania

Divisional Artillery: *New York Light, 13th Battery; Pennsylvania Light, Battery E*

THIRD DIVISION: Maj. Gen Daniel Butterfield; Brig. Gen William T. Ward
First Brigade: Brig. Gen William T. Ward; Col. Benjamin Harrison
102nd Illinois • 105th Illinois • 129th Illinois • 70th Indiana • 79th Ohio

Second Brigade: Col. John Coburn
20th Connecticut • 33rd Indiana • 85th Indiana • 19th Michigan
22nd Wisconsin

Third Brigade: Col. James Wood
20th Connecticut • 33rd Massachusetts • 136th New York • 55th Ohio
73rd Ohio • 26th Wisconsin

Reserve Brigade: Col. Joseph W. Burke; Col. Heber Le Favour
10th Ohio • 9th Michigan • 22nd Michigan

Divisional Artillery: *1st Michigan Light, Battery I • 1st Ohio Light, Battery C*

Pontoniers: Col. George P. Buell
58th Indiana • Pontoon Battalion

Ammunition Train Guard: Capt. Gershom M. Barber
1st Battalion Ohio Sharpshooters

Siege Artillery: Capt. Arnold Sutermeister
11th Indiana Battery

CAVALRY CORPS: Brig. Gen. Washington Elliott
FIRST DIVISION: Brig. Gen. Edward M. McCook
First Brigade: Col. Joseph B. Dorr
8th Iowa • 4th Kentucky Mounted Infantry • 2nd Michigan • 1st Tennessee

Second Brigade: Col. Oscar H. LaGrange; Lt. Col. James W. Stewart; Lt. Col. Horace P. Lamson
2nd Indiana • 4th Indiana • 1st Wisconsin

Third Brigade: Col. Louis D. Watkins; Col. John K. Faulkner
4th Kentucky • 6th Kentucky • 7th Kentucky

Divisional Artillery: *18th Indiana Battery*

SECOND DIVISION: Brig. Gen. Kenner Garrard
First Brigade: Col. Robert H. G. Minty
4th Michigan • 7th Pennsylvania • 4th U. S.

Second Brigade: Col. Eli Long
1st Ohio • 3rd Ohio • 4th Ohio

Third Brigade (Mounted Infantry): Col. John T. Wilder; Col. Abram O. Miller
98th Illinois • 123rd Illinois • 17th Indiana • 72nd Indiana

Divisional Artillery: *Chicago Board of Trade Battery*

THIRD DIVISION: Brig. Gen. Judson Kilpatrick; Col. Eli H. Murray; Col. William W. Lowe

First Brigade: Lt. Col. Robert Klein
3rd Indiana • 5th Iowa

Second Brigade: Col. Charles C. Smith; Maj. Thomas W. Sanderson
8th Indiana • 2nd Kentucky • 10th Ohio

Third Brigade: Col. Eli H. Murray; Col. Smith D. Adkins
92nd Illinois Mounted Infantry • 3rd Kentucky • 5th Kentucky

Divisional Artillery: *10thWisconsin Battery*

ARMY OF THE TENNESSEE
Maj. Gen. James B. McPherson

Chief of Artillery: Capt. Andrew Hickenlooper
Medical Director: Surgeon John Moore
Chief Engineer: Capt. Chauncey B. Reese

FIFTEENTH CORPS: Maj. Gen. John A. Logan
FIRST DIVISION: Brig. Gen. Peter J. Osterhaus; Brig. Gen. Charles R. Woods
First Brigade: Brig. Gen. Charles R. Woods
26th Iowa • 30th Iowa • 27th Missouri • 76th Ohio

Second Brigade: Col. James A. Williamson
4th Iowa • 9th Iowa • 25th Iowa • 31st Iowa

Third Brigade: Col. Hugo Wangelin
3rd Missouri • 12th Missouri • 17th Missouri • 29th Missouri • 31st Missouri • 32nd Missouri

Divisional Artillery: *2nd Missouri Light, Battery F • Ohio Light, 4th Battery*

SECOND DIVISION: Brig. Gen. Morgan L. Smith
First Brigade: Brig. Gen. Giles A. Smith
55th Illinois • 111th Illinois • 116th Illinois • 127th Illinois 6th Missouri • 8th Missouri • 30th Ohio • 57th Ohio

Second Brigade: Brig. Gen. Joseph Lightburn
111th Illinois • 83rd Indiana • 30th Ohio • 37th Ohio • 47th Ohio 53rd Ohio   54th Ohio

Divisional Artillery: Capt. Francis DeGress
1st Illinois Light, Battery A • *1st Illinois Light, Battery B* • *1st Illinois Light, Battery H*

THIRD DIVISION: Brig. Gen. William Harrow
First Brigade: Col. Reuben Williams
26th Illinois • *48th Illinois* • *90th Illinois* • *12th Indiana* • *99th Indiana*
100th Indiana • *15th Michigan* • *70th Ohio*

Second Brigade: Brig. Gen. Charles C. Walcutt
40th Illinois • *103rd Illinois* • *97th Indiana* • *6th Iowa* • *46th Ohio*

Third Brigade: Col. John M. Oliver
48th Illinois • *99th Indiana* • *15th Michigan* • *70th Ohio*

Divisional Artillery: Capt. Henry H. Griffiths; Maj. John T. Cheney
1st Illinois Light, Battery F • *Iowa Light, 1st Battery*

SIXTEENTH CORPS: Maj. Gen. Grenville M. Dodge
SECOND DIVISION: Brig. Gen. Thomas W. Sweeny
First Brigade: Brig. Gen. Elliott W. Rice
52nd Illinois • *66th Indiana* • *2nd Iowa* • *7th Iowa*

Second Brigade: Col. Patrick E. Burke; Lt. Col. Robert N. Adams; Col.
August Mersy
9th Illinois Mounted Infantry • *12th Illinois* • *66th Illinois* • *81st Ohio*

Third Brigade: Col. Moses E. Bane
7th Illinois • *50th Illinois* • *57th Illinois* • *39th Iowa*

Divisional Artillery: Capt. Frederick Welker
1st Michigan Light, Battery B • *1st Missouri Light, Battery H* • *1st Missouri
Light, Battery I*

FOURTH DIVISION: Brig. Gen. James C. Veatch; Brig. Gen. John W. Fuller
First Brigade: Brig. Gen. John W. Fuller
64th Illinois • *18th Missouri* • *27th Ohio* • *39th Ohio*

Second Brigade: Brig. Gen. John W. Sprague
35th New Jersey • 43rd Ohio • 63rd Ohio • 25th Wisconsin

Third Brigade: Col. William T. C. Grower
10th Illinois • 25th Indiana • 17th New York • 32nd Wisconsin

Divisional Artillery: Capt. Jerome B. Burrows; Capt. George Robinson
1st Michigan Light, Battery C • Ohio Light, 14th Battery • 2nd U. S., Battery F

SEVENTEENTH ARMY CORPS: Maj. Gen. Francis P. Blair
THIRD DIVISION: Brig. Gen. Mortimer D. Leggett
First Brigade: Brig. Gen. Manning F. Force
20th Illinois • 30th Illinois • 31st Illinois • 12th Wisconsin • 16th Wisconsin

Second Brigade: Col. Robert K. Scott
20th Ohio • 32nd Ohio • 68th Ohio • 78th Ohio

Third Brigade: Col. Adam G. Malloy
17th Wisconsin • Worden's Battalion

Divisional Artillery: Capt. William S. Williams
1st Illinois Light, Battery D • 1st Michigan Light, Battery H • Ohio Light, 3rd Battery

FOURTH DIVISION: Brig. Gen. Walter Q. Gresham
First Brigade: Col. William L. Sanderson
32nd Illinois • 53rd Illinois • 23rd Indiana • 53rd Indiana • 3rd Iowa (3 companies) 32nd Ohio • 12th Wisconsin

Second Brigade: Col. George C. Rogers; Col. Isaac C. Pugh
14th Illinois • 15th Illinois • 32nd Illinois • 41st Illinois • 53rd Illinois

Third Brigade: Col. William Hall
11th Iowa • 13th Iowa • 15th Iowa • 16th Iowa

Divisional Artillery: Capt. Edward Spear
2nd Illinois Light, Battery F • Minnesota Light, 1st Battery • 1st Missouri Light, Battery C • Ohio Light, 10th Battery • Ohio Light, 15th Battery

ARMY OF THE OHIO
Maj. Gen. John M. Schofield

TWENTY-THIRD CORPS: Maj. Gen. Jacob D. Cox

FIRST DIVISION: Brig. Gen. Alvin P. Hovey
First Brigade: Col. Richard Barter
120th Indiana • 124th Indiana • 128th Indiana
Second Brigade: Col. John Q. McQuiston; Col. Peter T. Swaine
123rd Indiana • 129th Indiana • 130th Indiana • 99th Ohio

Divisional Artillery: *Indiana Light, 23rd Battery • Indiana Light, 24th Battery*

SECOND DIVISION: Brig. Gen. Henry M. Judah; Brig. Gen Milo S. Hascall
First Brigade: Brig. Gen. Nathaniel C. McLean; Brig. Gen. Joseph A. Cooper
80th Indiana • 91st Indiana • 13th Kentucky • 25th Michigan • 45th Ohio 3rd Tennessee • 6th Tennessee

Second Brigade: Brig. Gen. Milo S. Hascall; Col. John R. Bond; Col. William E. Hobson
107th Illinois • 80th Indiana • 13th Kentucky • 23rd Michigan • 45th Ohio 111th Ohio • 118th Ohio

Third Brigade: Col. Silas A. Strickland
14th Kentucky • 20th Kentucky • 27th Kentucky • 50th Ohio

Divisional Artillery: Capt. Joseph C. Shields
Indiana Light, 22nd Battery • 1st Michigan Light, Battery F • Ohio Light, 19th Battery

THIRD DIVISION: Brig. Gen. Jacob D. Cox; Col. James W. Reilly
First Brigade: Col. James W. Reilly; Maj. James W. Gault
112th Illinois • 16th Kentucky • 100th Ohio • 104th Ohio • 8th Tennessee

Second Brigade: Brig. Gen. Mahlon D. Manson; Col. John S. Hurt; Col. Milo S. Hascall; Col. John S. Casement; Col. Daniel Cameron
65th Illinois • 63rd Indiana • 65th Indiana • 24th Kentucky 103rd Ohio • 5th Tennessee

Third Brigade: Brig. Gen. Nathaniel McLean; Col. Robert K. Byrd
11th Kentucky • 12th Kentucky • 1st Tennessee • 5th Tennessee

Dismounted Cavalry Brigade: Col. Eugene W. Crittenden
16th Illinois • 12th Kentucky

Divisional Artillery: Maj. Henry W. Wells
Indiana Light, 15th Battery • 1st Ohio Light, Battery D

STONEMAN'S CAVALRY DIVISION: Maj. Gen. George Stoneman
First Brigade: Col. Israel Garrard
9th Michigan • 7th Ohio

Second Brigade: Col. James Biddle
16th Illinois • 5th Indiana • 6th Indiana • 12th Kentucky

Third Brigade: Col. Horace Capron
14th Illinois • 8th Michigan • McLaughlin's Ohio Squadron

Independent Brigade: Col. Alexander W. Holeman
1st Kentucky • 11th Kentucky

Divisional Artillery: Capt. Alexander Hardy
24th Indiana Battery

ARMY OF TENNESSEE
Gen. John B. Hood

Chief of Staff: Brig. Gen. William W. Mackall; Brig. Gen. Francis A. Shoup
Chief of Artillery: Brig. Gen. Francis A. Shoup; Col. Robert F. Beckham
Chief Engineer: Lt. Col. Stephen W. Presstman; Maj. Martin L. Smith
Medical Director: Surg.-Maj. A. J. Foard

HARDEE'S CORPS: Lt. Gen. William J. Hardee
CHEATHAM'S DIVISION: Maj. Gen. Benjamin F. Cheatham
Maney's Brigade: Brig. Gen. George E. Maney; Col. Francis M. Walker
*1st & 27th Tennessee • 4th Confederate • 6th & 9th Tennessee
41st Tennessee • 50th Tennessee • 24th Tennessee Battalion*

Strahl's Brigade: Brig. Gen. Otho F. Strahl
4th & 5th Tennessee • 19th Tennessee • 24th Tennessee • 31st Tennessee
33rd Tennessee

Wright's Brigade: Col. John C. Carter
8th Tennessee • 16th Tennessee • 28th Tennessee • 38th Tennessee
51st & 52nd Tennessee

Vaughan's Brigade: Brig. Gen. Alfred J. Vaughan; Col. Michael
Magevney
11th Tennessee • 12th & 47th Tennessee • 29th Tennessee • 13th & 154th Tennessee

CLEBURNE'S DIVISION: Maj. Gen. Patrick R. Cleburne
Polk's Brigade: Brig. Gen. Lucius E. Polk
1st & 15th Arkansas • 5th Confederate • 2nd Tennessee • 35th Tennessee
48th Tennessee (Nixon's regiment)

Govan's Brigade: Brig. Gen. Daniel C. Govan
2nd & 24th Arkansas • 5th & 13th Arkansas • 6th & 7th Arkansas
8th & 19th Arkansas • 3rd Confederate

Lowrey's Brigade: Brig. Gen. Mark P. Lowrey
16th Alabama • 33rd Alabama • 45th Alabama • 32nd Mississippi
45th Mississippi

Granbury's Brigade: Brig. Gen. Hiram B. Granbury
6th Texas • 7th Texas • 10th Texas • 15th Texas Cavalry (dismounted)
17th & 18th Texas Cavalry (dismounted) • 24th & 25th Texas Cavalry (dismounted)

BATE'S DIVISION: Maj. Gen. William B. Bate
Tyler's Brigade: Brig. Gen. Thomas B. Smith
37th Georgia • 4th Georgia Battalion Sharpshooters • 10th Tennessee • 20th
Tennessee • 30th Tennessee • 15th & 37th Tennessee

Lewis's Brigade: Brig. Gen. Joseph H. Lewis
2nd Kentucky • 4th Kentucky • 5th Kentucky • 6th Kentucky • 9th Kentucky

Finley's Brigade: Brig. Gen. Jesse J. Finley
1st Florida Cavalry (dismounted) • *1st & 4th Florida* • *3rd Florida*
6th Florida • *7th Florida*

WALKER'S DIVISION: Maj. Gen. William H. T. Walker
Mercer's Brigade: Brig. Gen. Hugh W. Mercer
1st Volunteer Georgia • *54th Georgia* • *57th Georgia* • *63rd Georgia*

Gist's Brigade: Brig. Gen. States R. Gist
8th Georgia Battalion • *46th Georgia* • *16th South Carolina* • *24th South Carolina*

Jackson's Brigade: Brig. Gen. John K. Jackson
1st Georgia Confederate • *5th Georgia* • *47th Georgia* • *65th Georgia*
5th Mississippi • *8th Mississippi* • *2nd Georgia Battalion Sharpshooters*

Stevens's Brigade: Brig. Gen. Clement H. Stevens
25th Georgia • *29th Georgia* • *30th Georgia* • *66th Georgia* • *1st Georgia*
Battalion Sharpshooters • *26th Georgia Battalion*

HARDEE'S CORPS ARTILLERY: Col. Melancthon Smith
Hoxton's Battalion: Maj. Llewelyn Hoxton
Alabama Battery • *Marion (Florida) Light Artillery* • *Mississippi Battery*

Hotchkiss's Battalion: Maj. Thomas R. Hotchkiss
Arkansas Battery • *Semple's (Alabama) Battery* • *Warren (Mississippi) Light Artillery*

Martin's Battalion: Maj. Robert Martin
Bledsoe's (Missouri) Battery • *Ferguson's (South Carolina) Battery*
Howell's (Georgia) Battery

Cobb's Battalion: Maj. Robert Cobb
Cobb's (Kentucky) Battery • *Johnston (Tennessee) Artillery*
Washington (Louisiana) Light Artillery

HOOD'S CORPS: Maj. Gen. Benjamin F. Cheatham; Lt. Gen.
Stephen D. Lee

HINDMAN'S DIVISION: Maj. Gen. Thomas C. Hindman; Brig. Gen. John C. Brown

Deas's Brigade: Brig. Gen. Zachariah C. Deas
19th Alabama • 22nd Alabama • 25th Alabama • 39th Alabama
50th Alabama • 17th Alabama Battalion Sharpshooters

Manigault's Brigade: Brig. Gen. Arthur M. Manigault
24th Alabama • 28th Alabama • 34th Alabama • 10th South Carolina
19th South Carolina

Walthall's Brigade: Brig. Gen. Edward C. Walthall; Col. Samuel Benton
24th & 27th Mississippi • 29th, 30th and 34th Mississippi

Tucker's Brigade: Brig. Gen. William F. Tucker; Col. Jacob H. Sharp
7th Mississippi • 9th Mississippi • 10th Mississippi • 41st Mississippi
44th Mississippi • 9th Mississippi Battalion Sharpshooters

STEVENSON'S DIVISION: Maj. Gen. Carter L. Stevenson
Brown's Brigade: Brig. Gen. John C. Brown; Col. Joseph C. Palmer
3rd Tennessee • 18th Tennessee • 26th Tennessee • 32nd Tennessee
45th & 23rd Tennessee Battalion

Cumming's Brigade: Brig. Gen. Alfred Cumming
34th Georgia • 36th Georgia • 39th Georgia • 56th Georgia

Reynolds's Brigade: Brig. Gen. Alexander W. Reynolds
58th North Carolina • 60th North Carolina • 54th Virginia • 63rd Virginia

Pettus's Brigade: Brig. Gen. Edmund W. Pettus
20th Alabama • 23rd Alabama • 30th Alabama • 31st Alabama • 46th Alabama

STEWART'S DIVISION: Maj. Gen. Alexander P. Stewart; Maj. Gen. Henry D. Clayton
Stovall's Brigade: Brig. Gen. Marcellus A. Stovall; Col. Abda Johnson
40th Georgia • 41st Georgia • 42nd Georgia • 43rd Georgia • 52nd Georgia

Clayton's Brigade: Brig. Gen. Henry D. Clayton; Brig. Gen. James T. Holtzclaw
18th Alabama • 32nd & 58th Alabama • 36th Alabama • 38th Alabama

Gibson's Brigade: Brig. Gen. Randall L. Gibson
*1st Louisiana • 13th Louisiana • 16th & 25th Louisiana • 19th Louisiana
20th Louisiana • 4th Louisiana Battalion • 14th Louisiana Battalion Sharpshooters*

Baker's Brigade: Brig. Gen. Alpheus Baker
37th Alabama • 40th Alabama • 42nd Alabama

HOOD'S CORPS ARTILLERY: Col. Robert F. Beckham; Lt. Col. James H. Hallonquist
Courtney's Battalion: Maj. Alfred R. Courtney
Alabama Battery • Douglas's (Texas) Battery • Alabama Battery

Eldridge's Battalion: Maj. John W. Eldridge
Eufaula (Alabama) Artillery • Louisiana Battery • Mississippi Battery
Johnston's Battalion: Maj. John W. Johnston; Cap. Max. Van Den Corput
Cherokee (Georgia) Artillery • Stephens (Georgia) Light Artillery • Tennessee Battery

ARMY OF TENNESSEE ARTILLERY RESERVE
Palmer's Battalion: Maj. Joseph Palmer
Georgia Battery • Alabama Battery • Georgia Battery

Williams's Battalion: Lt. Col. Samuel C. Williams
*Barbour (Alabama) Artillery • Jefferson (Mississippi) Artillery
Nottoway (Virginia) Artillery*

Waddell's Battalion: Maj. James F. Waddell
*Emery's (Alabama) Battery • Bellamy's (Alabama) Battery
Barret's (Missouri) Battery*

CAVALRY CORPS: Maj. Gen. Joseph Wheeler
MARTIN'S DIVISION: Maj. Gen. William T. Martin
Morgan's Brigade: Brig. Gen. John T. Morgan
1st Alabama • 3rd Alabama • 4th Alabama • 7th Alabama • 51st Alabama

Iverson's Brigade: Brig. Gen. Alfred Iverson
1st Georgia • 2nd Georgia • 3rd Georgia • 4th Georgia • 6th Georgia

KELLY'S DIVISION: Brig. Gen. John H. Kelly
Allen's Brigade: Brig. Gen. William W. Allen
3rd Confederate • 8th Confederate • 10th Confederate • 12th Confederate

Dibrell's Brigade: Col. George G. Dibrell
4th Tennessee • 8th Tennessee • 9th Tennessee • 10th Tennessee • 11th Tennessee

Williams' Brigade: Brig. Gen John S. Williams
1st Kentucky • 2nd Kentucky • 9th Kentucky • 2nd Kentucky Battalion
Allison's (Tennessee) Squadron • detachment Hamilton's (Tennessee) Battalion

Hannon's Brigade: Col. Moses W. Hannon
53rd Alabama • 24th Alabama Battalion

HUMES'S DIVISION: Brig Gen. William Y. C. Humes
Humes's Brigade: Col. James T. Wheeler
1st Tennessee • 2nd Tennessee • 5th Tennessee • 9th Tennessee Battalion

Harrison's Brigade: Col. Thomas H. Harrison
3rd Arkansas • 8th Texas • 11th Texas

CAVALRY CORPS ARTILLERY: Lt. Col. Felix H. Robertson
Ferrell's (Georgia) Battery (1 section) • Huwald's (Tennessee) Battery
Tennessee Battery Wiggins' (Arkansas) Battery

ARMY OF MISSISSIPPI / STEWART'S CORPS
Lt. Gen. Alexander P. Stewart

Chief of Artillery: Lt. Col. Samuel C. Williams

LORING'S DIVISION: Maj. Gen. William W. Loring;
Brig. Gen. Winfield S. Featherston
Featherston's Brigade: Brig. Gen. Winfield S. Featherston
3rd Mississippi • 22nd Mississippi • 31st Mississippi • 33rd Mississippi
40th Mississippi • 1st Mississippi Battalion Sharpshooters

Adams's Brigade: Brig. Gen. John Adams
6th Mississippi • 14th Mississippi • 15th Mississippi • 20th Mississippi
23rd Mississippi • 43rd Mississippi

Scott's Brigade: Brig. Gen. Thomas M. Scott
27th Alabama • 35th Alabama • 49th Alabama • 55th Alabama
57th Alabama • 12th Louisiana

Divisional Artillery/Myrick's Battalion: Maj. John D. Myrick
Mississippi Battery • Lookout Tennessee Battery • Pointe Coupee Battery

FRENCH'S DIVISION: Maj. Gen. Samuel G. French
Ector's Brigade: Brig. Gen. Mathew D. Ector
29th North Carolina • 39th North Carolina • 9th Texas • 10th Texas Cavalry
(dismounted) 14th Texas Cavalry (dismounted) • 32nd Texas Cavalry (dismounted)

Cockrell's Brigade: Brig. Gen. Francis M. Cockrell; Col. Elijah Gates
1st & 4th Missouri • 2nd & 6th Missouri • 3rd & 5th Missouri
1st & 3rd Missouri Cavalry (dismounted)

Sears's Brigade: Brig. Gen. Claudius W. Sears
4th Mississippi • 35th Mississippi • 36th Mississippi • 46th Mississippi
7th Mississippi Battalion

Divisional Artillery/Storrs's Battalion: Maj. George S. Storrs
Ward's (Alabama) Battery • Hoskins' (Mississippi) Battery • Guibor's (Missouri) Battery

WALTHALL'S DIVISION: Maj. Gen. Edward C. Walthall
Reynolds's Brigade: Brig. Gen. Daniel H. Reynolds
1st Arkansas Mounted Rifles (dismounted) • 2nd Arkansas Mounted Rifles
(dismounted) • 4th Arkansas • 9th Arkansas • 25th Arkansas

Cantey's Brigade: Brig. Gen. James Cantey; Col. Edward A. O'Neal
17th Alabama • 26th Alabama • 29th Alabama • 37th Mississippi
Battalion Alabama Sharpshooters

Quarles's Brigade: Brig. Gen. William A. Quarles
1st Alabama • 4th Alabama • 30th Louisiana • 42nd Tennessee
46th & 55th Tennessee 48th Tennessee • 49th Tennessee • 53rd Tennessee

Divisional Artillery/Preston's Battalion: Maj. William C. Preston
Yates's (Mississippi) Battery • Tarrant's (Alabama) Battery • Selden's (Alabama) Battery

CAVALRY DIVISION: Brig. Gen. William H. Jackson
Armstrong's Brigade: Brig. Gen. Frank C. Armstrong
1st Mississippi • 2nd Mississippi • 28th Mississippi • Ballentine's (Mississippi) Regiment

Ross's Brigade: Brig. Gen. Lawrence S. Ross
3rd Texas • 6th Texas • 9th Texas • 1st Texas Legion

Ferguson's Brigade: Brig. Gen. Samuel W. Ferguson
*2nd Alabama • 56th Alabama • 9th Mississippi • 11th Mississippi
12th Mississippi Battalion*

Divisional Artillery: Capt. John Waties
*Columbus (Georgia) Light Artillery • Clark (Missouri) Artillery
Waties's (South Carolina) Battery*

ENGINEER TROOPS: Lt. Col. Stephen W. Presstman;
Maj. Gen. Martin L. Smith
Companies A-D, F, G • Sappers & Miners

GEORGIA MILITIA
Maj. Gen. Gustavus W. Smith

FIRST DIVISION
First Brigade: Brig. Gen. Reuben W. Carswell
1st Regiment • 2nd Regiment • 3rd Regiment

Second Brigade: Brig. Gen. Pleasant J. Philips
4th Regiment • 5th Regiment • 6th Regiment

Third Brigade: Brig. Gen. Charles D. Anderson
7th Regiment • 8th Regiment • 9th Regiment

Fourth Brigade: Brig. Gen. Henry K. McCay
10th Regiment • 11th Regiment • 12th Regiment

Suggested Reading

BY STEPHEN DAVIS

The Day Dixie Died: The Battle of Atlanta
Gary Ecelbarger
St. Martin's Press (2010)
ISBN: 978-0-312-56399-8

Hood's plan for a Jacksonian flank assault fell apart, but his attacking battle of July 22 was nonetheless the closest thing he had to a battlefield victory during the campaign. Ecelbarger's title is hyperbolic, but his book is welcome as the first to solely treat this engagement. He does it very competently.

Sherman's Horsemen: Union Cavalry Operations in the Atlanta Campaign
David Evans
Indiana University Press (1996)
ISBN: 0-253-32963-9

Sherman, like many generals on both sides, placed too much confidence in his cavalry's ability to achieve meaningful results. (As we have seen, he was sorely disappointed by McCook's and Stoneman's failure to cut the Macon & Western Railroad.) Evans thoroughly explains every Union cavalry initiative during July-August. It's the only source I have found, for example, that measures the extent of damage to the Montgomery & West Point Railroad by Lovell Rousseau's raiders (26 miles).

The Battle of Ezra Church and the Struggle for Atlanta
Earl J. Hess
University of North Carolina Press (2015)
ISBN: 978-1-4696-2241-5

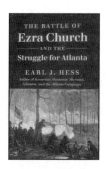

Finally, trifecta! Hess's is an excellent study. Along with Ecelbarger's and Jenkins's, we have solid books on all three of the major battles fought around Atlanta in July 1864.

The Battle of Peach Tree Creek: Hood's First Sortie, July 20, 1864
Robert D. Jenkins
Mercer University Press (2013)
ISBN: 9-780881-463965

Jenkins's interest in this battle stemmed from his great-great grandfather, a soldier in the 31st Mississippi who fought at Peachtree Creek. His idea first to write a regimental history blossomed into this, the first book to explain the battle of July 20. I don't agree with Bob on everything— he's a friend, and he knows this—especially on Johnston's alleged authorship of Hood's battle plan. But on this big engagement, Jenkins's thorough research and detailed writing make this the only book to turn to.

About the Author

Stephen Davis of Atlanta has been a Civil War buff since the fourth grade. He attended Emory University and studied under the renowned Civil War historian Bell Wiley. After a master's degree in American history from the University of North Carolina at Chapel Hill, he taught high school for a few years, then earned his Ph.D. at Emory, where he concentrated on the theme of the Civil War in Southern literature.

Steve is the author of a survey of the Atlanta campaign, *Atlanta Will Fall: Sherman, John Johnston and the Heavy Yankee Battalions* (2001). His book *What the Yankees Did to Us: Sherman's Bombardment and Wrecking of Atlanta* was published by Mercer University Press in 2012. In a review in *Civil War News*, Ted Savas calls Steve's book "by far the most well-researched, thorough, and detailed account ever written about the 'wrecking' of Atlanta."

Steve served as book review editor for *Blue & Gray* magazine from 1984 to 2005, and is the author of more than a hundred articles in such scholarly and popular publications as *Civil War Times Illustrated* and the *Georgia Historical Quarterly*. He also served as the historian/content partner for the Civil War Trust's Atlanta Campaign Battle App, produced in 2013-14.

In 2015, Steve served as a speaker and consultant for the television documentary "When Georgia Howled: Sherman on the March," a joint production of the Atlanta History Center and Georgia Public Broadcasting. Steve is also a popular speaker at Civil War round tables and historical societies. His favorite event was a couple of years ago when he addressed President and Mrs. Carter and family on the role of Copenhill (the Carter Center) in the battle of Atlanta.

Steve is author of a companion volume to this book, also part of the Emerging Civil War Series:

A Long and Bloody Task:
The Atlanta Campaign from Dalton Through
Kennesaw Mountain to the Chattahoochee River
May 5-July 18, 1864